SENSATE FOCUS IN SEX THERAPY

The Illustrated Manual

Linda Weiner and Constance Avery-Clark

Routledge
Taylor & Francis Group

NEW YORK AND LONDON

First published 2017

by Routledge

711 Third Avenue, New York, NY 10017

and by Routledge

2 Park Square, Milton Park, Abingdon, Oxon, OX14 4RN

Routledge is an imprint of the Taylor & Francis Group, an informa business

Library of Congress Cataloging-in-Publication Data
Weiner, Linda, author. | Avery-Clark, Constance, author.
Sensate focus in sex therapy : the illustrated manual / by Linda Weiner
and Constance Avery-Clark. New York, NY : Routledge, 2017.
Includes bibliographical references and index.
LCCN 2016042936| ISBN 9781138642355 (hbk : alk. paper) |
ISBN 9781138642362 (pbk : alk. paper) | ISBN 9781315630038 (ebk)
MESH: Marital Therapy–methods | Couples Therapy–methods |
Sexual Dysfunctions, Psychological–therapy | Sexual Dysfunction, Physiological–therapy
LCC RC488.5
NLM WM 430.5.M3
DDC 616.89/1562–dc23
LC record available at https://lccn.loc.gov/2016042936

ISBN: 978-1-138-64235-5 (hbk)
ISBN: 978-1-138-64236-2 (pbk)
ISBN: 978-1-315-63003-8 (ebk)

Typeset in Zurich
by Out of House Publishing

To our mentors, William Masters, M.D., and Virginia Johnson, D.Sc. (Hon), whose intention it was to write a more detailed description of Sensate Focus but whose time was too short.

Contents

Contents

List of Illustrations

All illustrations © Karen Ann Jones, www.karenannjones.com/
Illustration photographer Mark Moore and Raymond Gehman

Foreword

Sensate Focus in Sex Therapy: The Illustrated Manual reconnects the reader with one of the hallmarks of the pioneering days of sex therapy: Sensate Focus. At its most basic, Sensate Focus is a technique to minimize performance anxiety and "spectatoring." It may be counter-intuitive to some on first consideration, but the very success of sexual pharmaceuticals, and their impact on sexual health delivery world-wide, makes this book a must-read for any health-care professional assisting people suffering from sexual disorders and concerns. Why? Medical approaches to sexual disorders are optimized when medical interventions are integrated with counseling. Understanding the rationale for non-demand experimentation and the basics of Sensate Focus can be a powerful weapon for anyone attempting to assist those who suffer, whether a sex educator nurse practitioner, physician, or psychotherapist. Sexual disorders and concerns are multi-determined by a host of varied biological and psychosocial-behavioral and cultural factors. Yet, those who suffer from sexual disorders all have an underlying concern and anxiety about disappointing themselves and their partner. Sensate Focus techniques can help a person learn how to manage those issues and that is the focus of this volume.

I was honored when Linda Weiner and Constance Avery-Clark, earlier this year, expressed their eagerness for me to write a foreword for this volume, that was inspired by the work of my former mentor and colleague Helen Kaplan, and my friends Bill Masters and Gini Johnson. All three of them did so much for our profession and society in general. I certainly owe my own career of over 40 years to them. This is a book whose time has come. How might that be? In Masters and Johnson's preface to the 1970 landmark, *Human Sexual Inadequacy* (a book that launched sex therapy and introduced the world to Sensate Focus) they wrote: "It is to be hoped that human sexual inadequacy, both the entity and this book would be rendered obsolete in the next decade" (Masters & Johnson, 1970, pp. v). Despite the tremendous progress that has been made over ensuing decades, their hopes could not have been more unrealized as the parade of distressed individuals seeking assistance daily all over the world for relief from the suffering caused by their sexual problems continues to this day. Of course there is no one cure, but *Sensate Focus in Sex Therapy: The Illustrated Manual* provides a guide to familiarize (re-intro-duce) novice sex therapists and experienced master clinicians, as well as the public at large, to a technique that has universal application in almost every case where sexual symptoms exist.

This book has a number of strengths, but I want to highlight a few for the reader. Most important to the professionals reading this book, the authors advocate for and practice a type of communication that is key to good diagnosis and treatment. First quoting Marcel Proust, "Be precise, my dear, be precise," the authors elaborate: "As therapists we must be Proustian in our measured attention to the details of sensation descriptions so that our clients will want to divulge everything down to minute details." The key to a good sex status (focused sex history) is obtaining the details, and that can be part of almost every consultation. For the novice therapist in particular, explicit and elaborate explanations of the why and how to give instructions for Sensate Focus is quite useful. The authors explore the theory behind reducing performance anxiety. This is a common cause of sexual disorders and one that is almost always a factor in the maintenance of sexual disorders regardless of whether a pharmaceutical and/or sexual counseling has been initiated. Both the why and the how to initiate Sensate Focus instructions are provided, with sensitive consideration for diverse patient populations and varying overlapping disorders. Again, the emphasis on providing precise and vivid descriptions and seeking the same back from clients is something we all must be reminded to do continuously.

For novice and experienced clinicians alike, Weiner and Avery-Clark explore the management of common problems and resistance to both the outcome and process of Sensate Focus. That in-depth discussion includes, but is not limited to, non-compliance, boredom, lack of spontaneity, ticklishness, feeling nothing, sexual frustration, confusion about, and difficulties with either/or Sensate Focus concepts and instructions. In almost all cases the process involves the clients learning to recognize and acknowledge their anxiety, communicate it, but then move beyond it by refocusing their attention productively. All are also reminded of the importance of patience when seeking change and of the necessity to appreciate systematic approximation and embracing how small iterative steps can lead to longer lasting confidence and success. Explanation of how to manage distractions through cognitive-behavioral mindfulness techniques should especially appeal to those practicing this currently popular approach with its many adherents.

Of course the illustrations themselves, like those in Helen Kaplan's *The Illustrated Manual of Sex Therapy* (1975; 1987), help inspire this current book and offer so much to both the public and professionals alike. However, unlike Helen's own pioneering work, the interpretive non-traditional illustrations illuminate a broader application of Sensate Focus to a larger group of sexual concerns and a more diverse audience. That varied range is recognizable among the participants who are illustrated within themes that recognize aging, loss (mastectomy, leg prosthesis), and race. This naturally broadens the audience of the book's utility for use by professionals and those seeking self-help alike.

What all cognitive-behaviorally-oriented therapists know is that helping someone behave themselves into a new way of thinking and feeling is possible and rewarding for both clinician and client/patient. Weiner and Avery-Clark conclude their book with an acknowledgment of the primary nature of touch. What I have always loved about sex therapy is the fact that "mother nature" is on my side – that is always a good thing. All who read this book will benefit and find useful guidance in their efforts to make sex a positive force in both their personal and professional lives.

Michael A. Perelman, Ph.D.
Co-Director, Human Sexuality Program
Clinical Professor Emeritus of Psychology in Psychiatry
Former Clinical Professor of Reproductive Medicine & Urology
Weill Cornell Medicine | NewYork-Presbyterian

Acknowledgments

This book could never have been written without the support and encouragement of many sex therapists who reported the need for an in-depth description of the purposes and specific instructions for the Sensate Focus touching experiences that represent the foundation of sex therapy. Many of these supporters took an online survey of their use of Sensate Focus in their practices with varied populations, and they convinced us that this modality is neither out of practice nor ineffective. It has merely been awaiting manualization and the addition of the compiled wisdom of practitioners over the last 30 years. Among the most avid supporters has been Barry McCarthy, Ph.D., who read one of the later drafts and spent considerable time giving feedback and suggestions. We are indebted to Michael Perelman, Ph.D., for his early interest and support, editorial suggestions, and for offering to write the Foreword. Susan Stiritz, Ph.D., MBA, MSW, also read a later draft and provided helpful input. Others who supported this project from inception include Michael Plaut, Ph.D., and Joanna Whitcup, Ph.D., to whom we owe our sincere appreciation. Many others provided us help with fact-checking regarding the use of Sensate Focus with varied populations with whom the authors had less familiarity. We thank you!

This project involved both the art of photographers and illustrators and also the willingness of models to complete our dream of following Dr. Helen Singer Kaplan's lead in creating visual representations of both the beauty of human sexuality and the practical application of Sensate Focus. Luck was with us when *National Geographic* photographer Raymond Gehman agreed to take the photographs, and Karen Ann Jones agreed to translate those photographs into the expressive illustrations contained in this book.

We would not even have begun a project like this nor found the energy and focus to see it through without the help of our superb publisher, Routledge, and our multi-talented Editor, Elizabeth Graber. She was the one who sold us on the idea in the first place, and kept us on task when deadlines loomed large.

We would not be complete in our acknowledgments without recognizing the hundreds of clients who have come our way over the last three and a half decades, seeking help and offering feedback on what is helpful for them when using Sensate Focus, and what is not. This is especially the case with our most challenged clients and clients from diverse backgrounds. They have taught us more than we have taught them about the nuances and modifications of Sensate Focus.

Chapter 1: Introduction

"Sexuality is not mere instinctuality; it is an indisputably creative power."

(Jung, 1966, para. 107)

Sex. So much has changed in the last 50 years since the publication of Masters and Johnson's *Human Sexual Response* (1966) and *Human Sexual Inadequacy* (1970). And so much has not. So much is easier. And so much is more complicated than ever.

Brief Overview of the Field of Sex Therapy

Thanks to the contributions of many different clinicians, researchers, and sexologists working with many more diverse populations than Masters and Johnson, we know a lot more about the physiological bases of sexuality and the biomedical sources of sexual concerns. We also know much more about psychological, relational, lifestyle, and cultural factors that contribute to sexual problems. Thanks to these same professionals, we know a lot more about ways to treat sexual distress and to improve sexual satisfaction across many populations, often requiring modifications in the original Masters and Johnson sex therapy and Sensate Focus protocols.

However, we are also aware that sexual functioning and its meaningfulness are so multidimensional that understanding just the physiology or just the psychology or just the cultural factors is not enough to explain many sexual problems and dissatisfactions. To add to the complexity, we also know that treating sexual concerns and dissatisfactions is not a simple matter of using this approach or that. We also know that many people are often still too uncomfortable to talk about their sexual concerns and to seek out professionals who can help them. This is unfortunate because we definitely know that sexuality specialists today have more tools to help individuals and couples experiencing sexual dysfunctions.

Why Are We Writing This Manual?

We hope that *Sensate Focus in Sex Therapy: The Illustrated Manual* will help health professionals become more comfortable with and knowledgeable about how, when, and why to use the power of Sensate Focus. We anticipate that by making this manual available to clinicians and their potential clients, we will lessen the discomfort of people thinking about meeting with a health professional.

We are particularly excited about two additional and specific reasons for writing this manual. The first is *clarifying* Sensate Focus, both in theory and practical application. This is something that has never been done before. The second is *shining the spotlight back on the whole person*. The field of sex therapy appears to be gravitating towards what we believe is an overemphasis on the biological view, and we want to keep the psychological, relational, cultural, and spiritual work integrated *with* the biological.

Clarifying Sensate Focus

While there are many excellent publications on how to do sex therapy, there is nothing that has been published in any depth about the foundational centerpiece of sex therapy that is *Sensate Focus*. The main reason we want to publish this manual is to clarify one of the most powerful approaches to resolving sexual dysfunctions that is already in the hands of clinicians and has been for nearly 50 years. This deceptively simple, straightforward series of touching opportunities developed by William Masters and Virginia Johnson (1970) can have a profound impact on resolving sexual dysfunctions. It may also optimize the intimate and sexual relationship specifically, and enhance the overall relationship generally.

However, despite its power and the fact that Sensate Focus continues to be widely used by sex therapists (Weiner & Stiritz, 2014), and after more than three and a half decades of our practicing, presenting, and publishing on Sensate Focus, we realize this time-honored foundation of sex therapy remains confusing to many. It is often applied differently than what we believe makes it most effective practically, and differently than what makes its application consistent with its theoretical underpinnings. This has resulted in misunderstandings over the purpose, value, and procedures of Sensate Focus.

> Witkin … reflects the widespread objection to the Masters and Johnson [Sensate Focus] assignments – that they block spontaneity. Ironically, this is precisely their objective. The fact that this is not generally known arises from Masters and Johnson's way of presenting their work. Outside of participation in their full-time training program or attendance at their training seminars there is no way to become familiar with many of the essentials of their model …
>
> Not only has their model yet to be completely presented in published form, its deceptive simplicity has made it seem limited at best. This is a crucial misunderstanding. Masters and Johnson's therapy is a revolutionary departure, even from subsequently established approaches that are thought to be based on it and simply to go beyond it.
>
> (Apfelbaum, 1995, pp. 23–24)

On this basis, we have decided that a more complete, detailed, yet reader-friendly published manual on Sensate Focus is long overdue. That is the primary purpose of this *Illustrated Manual*. We are intending to cover all aspects of Sensate Focus, including both the practical details of its application so clinicians will know how to use it, and also its theoretical underpinnings in order to clear up any misunderstandings about its purpose. We hope that by including both the practical and the conceptual we will appeal to a variety of readers. New clinicians will find it helpful in the real world of therapy. More seasoned therapists may be intrigued with the historical perspective and become more confident about adding sexuality interventions into their practice. Sexuality professionals and other practitioners will find helpful suggestions for working with a wider variety of clients than was the case in the days of Masters and Johnson.

In doing this we hope to clarify how to apply Sensate Focus in a manner we believe to be most effective in the treatment setting. This is based on the more than 60 years of experience we have between the two of us. However, we are also hoping this manual will stimulate more research that will empirically and more rigorously validate our experience than has been the case up until now.

Addressing both the application and conceptual foundation of Sensate Focus is probably a reflection of the differences between the authors. Linda tends to look at sexual problems from a more practical perspective: "What do I need to suggest to clients to help them right now, and how can I put it in terms they will immediately understand?" This most likely comes from her educational and professional background as a systemic-oriented social worker and trainer. Constance often emphasizes the theoretical: "How can I help the clients understand the larger context of their concerns so they will become more interested in them, more motivated to work on them, and more motivated to continue with their progress?" This is probably associated with her education and training as a more depth- and Jungian-oriented clinical psychologist. Clearly both viewpoints are critical, and we hope that by working together we offer a comprehensive overview of Sensate Focus that will be both helpful and interesting.

Defining Sensate Focus and its Purpose

Sensate Focus is a set of touching suggestions that serves as a powerful therapeutic approach for helping people experiencing sexual concerns. While we will be focusing mainly on Sensate Focus with sexual dysfunctions, we will also be describing to a limited degree some of the effects Sensate Focus can have on greatly improving sexual intimacy and overall relationship satisfaction. We refer to the concepts and techniques for resolving sexual dysfunctions as *Sensate Focus 1*. We refer to concepts and techniques for enhancing intimacy and relationship satisfaction as *Sensate Focus 2*. We will discuss Sensate Focus 2 in more detail subsequently and we will distinguish Sensate Focus 1 and Sensate Focus 2 throughout this manual.

Detailing Instructions and Offering Illustrations

While Masters and Johnson acknowledged the lack of specific information on the use of Sensate Focus, they never published a precise description of the instructions. This manual will do just that. However, perhaps its most important contribution will be providing not just written instructions but also visual illustrations about how to use Sensate Focus. We have taken our inspiration from *The Illustrated Manual of Sex Therapy* (1975; 1987) by Helen Singer Kaplan. In it, Dr. Kaplan made a point of writing in a less academic style so her work would be more accessible to clinicians and laypersons alike. Perhaps even more significantly, she provided illustrations to both clarify the positions and activities used in sex therapy techniques and also to suggest "the beauty and humanity of sex":

> In the past ... I have had to rely on my verbal descriptions. Often these do not convey the various positions with sufficient clarity and I have had to make sketches to illustrate what I was asking them to do. On some occasions members of the staff have actually had to demonstrate some of the more difficult positions ... It is the objective of the drawings ... to provide clear illustrations for commonly suggested positions ... The drawings will, apart from merely illustrating specific positions, also, I hope, convey the beauty and humanity of sex, fundamentals to successful sex therapy.
>
> (Kaplan, 1987, p. 5)

1.1

The Beauty and Humanity of Sex

Shining the Spotlight Back on the Whole Person

Another reason we decided to publish this *Illustrated Manual* is to emphasize the need for a refocusing on the entirety of each client's experience. We do this by raising awareness of the history of Sensate Focus and the advances in modifications for more diverse populations. We are going to describe using Sensate Focus with people experiencing a variety of sexual dysfunctions, physical challenges, psychological concerns, relationship dynamics, lifestyle stressors, and value systems.

The field of sexology has become increasingly medicalized over the past several decades. It began with the contributions of Helen Singer Kaplan in the mid-1970s, and has been both helpful and not so helpful. There is no question that one of the most important advances in the sexuality field has been the development of medications and procedures to address sexual dysfunctions. We now have increasingly accurate medical assessments and interventions to help people who are experiencing hormonal, cardiovascular, neurological, anatomical, and illness-related problems affecting their sexual functioning.

However, we need a wake-up call because this same emphasis may demote sex therapists to a secondary rather than a collaborative role, or to no role at all. This is a big problem. While medical interventions are most useful for those clients who are experiencing medical or mixed etiologies, they do not address the psychosocial difficulties that arise even in cases where the primary etiology is medical. Many clinicians tell us, "Sexual dysfunction is inevitably complicated. It is multi-causal (biopsychosocial), multidimensional (psychological and interactional), and has multiple effects on the person, the partner, and their relationship" (Metz & McCarthy, 2012, p. 213). Despite this, eminently respected sex therapist and psychologist Michael Perelman notes,

> Regrettably and more rapidly than any sex therapist could imagine, the exaggerated mid-century notion that psychological problems caused most sexual dysfunctions was replaced by a media-fueled equally fallacious argument that sexual problems were almost exclusively the result of organic causes. Dismissed from the public discourse and all but forgotten was the truism that every sexual disorder, regardless of the severity of its organic etiology, also has a psychosocial component – if not causative, then certainly consequential.
>
> (Perelman, 2016, p. 40)

Nowhere is the influence of this emphasis on medicine and biology more evident than in the recent publication of the controversial *Diagnostic and Statistical Manual of Mental Disorders, Fifth Edition* (*DSM-5*) (American Psychiatric Association, 2015). In this bible of clinical diagnoses, the psychological, relationship, lifestyle, and social contributions to sexual dysfunctions have been relegated to "associated features": "One new exclusion criterion was added: the disorder should not be better explained by a 'nonsexual mental disorder, a consequence of severe relationship distress (e.g., partner violence) or other significant stressors'" (IsHak & Tobia, 2013, p. 2). This suggests that, according to the *DSM-5*, an individual's psychological disorders, a couple's significant relationship problems, or other significant lifestyle concerns may not be the primary diagnosable cause of sexual dysfunctions.

It is a rare case in which there is solely a medical component to a sexual dysfunction. Even if physiological problems contribute to the onset of the dysfunction, individual, relationship, and other psychosocial factors also often play a significant role in the origin of a sexual concern, and a much more significant role in maintaining the problem. For example, Perelman's (2009) *Sexual Tipping Point*® model reminds us of the mind–body connection.

> The Sexual Tipping Point® model depicts the continuously dynamic and variable nature of an individual's sexual response on a distribution curve … [It] easily illuminates the mind–body concept that mental factors can "turn you on" as well as "turn you off"; the same is true of the physical factors. Therefore, an individual's Sexual Tipping Point represents the cumulative impact of the interaction of a constitutionally established capacity to express a sexual response elicited by different types of stimulation as dynamically

impacted by various psychosocial-behavioral and cultural factors. An individual's threshold will vary somewhat from one sexual experience to another based on the proportional effect of all the different factors that determine their tipping point at a particular moment in time, with one factor or another dominating while others recede in importance.

(Perelman, 2016, pp. 40–41)

Perelman's model emphasizes the need to look at medical issues. However, it also reminds us not to let the popularity and apparent convenience of medical approaches overwhelm and distract us away from the role that the psychological, relational, and other factors play.

Stanley Althof, Executive Director of the Center for Sexual and Marital Health in South Florida, notes,

It seems odd that combined pharmacological and psychological treatment of sexual problems has not established itself as a mainstream intervention for either mental health clinicians or sexual health physicians who treat sexual problems ... Studies on combined medical and psychological therapy all demonstrate that combined treatment is superior to medical treatment alone.

(Althof, 2010, p. 125)

Throughout this manual we are going to be shining the spotlight back on the psychological, relationship, lifestyle, and cultural factors influencing sexual dysfunctions in order to rebalance the current trend towards medicalization. We believe strongly that the field is in danger of losing sight of the complexity, power, and mystery of sexuality if these variables are not re-emphasized and valued for the role they play.

What We Are Going to Leave to Others

As a result of our highlighting the psychosocial factors involved in sexual dysfunctions, we are going to leave it to other clinicians and researchers to elaborate on the details of sexual medicine, including pharmacology, tests, and treatments. For now and for the most part, we are also going to leave it to others to detail the multidisciplinary approach to treating sexual dysfunctions that weaves together the biomedical with the psychosocial.

We are not going to include a history of the field of sex therapy or all the various models developed by others who work with sexual dysfunctions. However, we do want to take this opportunity to acknowledge some of the professionals who have influenced our thinking and practice. Stanley Althof (2010) does an excellent job of describing a number of these paradigms as they have emerged over the years: Kaplan (1974) "integrated psychoanalytic theory with Masters and Johnson's cognitive behavioral understanding of sexual dysfunction" (p. 391). Linda De Villers and Heather Turgeon (2005) succinctly describe the behavioral model of Sensate Focus. Gerald Weeks and Nancy Gambescia (2009), and Katherine Hertlein (Hertlein & Weeks, 2009) emphasize an *Intersystem Model*, integrating individual, interactional, and intergenerational systems, and maintaining a focus on the couple during Sensate Focus. Tammy Nelson (2008) similarly emphasizes couples' interaction and communication, and incorporates an Imago therapeutic approach to physical contact. Stella Resnick (2012) reminds us of the importance of the mind–body interconnection in a Gestalt- and embodiment-oriented approach. Gina Ogden's (2001; 2013) many publications and work-shops also remind us of the significance of these interconnections as well as those with the heart and spirit, while Mark A. Michaels and Patricia Johnson (2006) celebrate the sacred-ness of the body from a Tantric perspective that suggests another way to build and store sexual energy. These are concepts and techniques that parallel or dovetail with Sensate Focus. Peggy Kleinplatz and A. Dana Ménard (2007), and Kleinplatz et al. (2009), increasingly emphasize the existential and experiential aspects of sexuality, and psychologist Christopher Aanstoos (2012) takes the experiential even farther by zeroing in on the phenomenology of sexual experiencing. These are but a few of the valuable models and perspectives offered by professionals in the field of sex therapy.

Although we will describe the modifications to sex therapy and Sensate Focus that are helpful when working with diverse populations, we obviously cannot cover them all. We had to make some hard choices. We hope this manual will offer practical details on the use of Sensate Focus suggestions and shine the light on the many creative adaptations other clini-cians have made to our understanding of its use with more diverse populations. We also want to prompt others to continue to develop, research, and elaborate on additional diversities and adaptations.

How to Read This Manual

We have tried to weave the more general and conceptual underpinnings of Sensate Focus together with its practical application. Some people prefer the former, some the latter. Some chapters are weighted more in one direction and some in the other.

The second chapter, *Sensate Focus*, is balanced between the theoretical and practical, and offers an overview of what the field of sex therapy is all about in general and what Sensate Focus is all about in particular. It also distinguishes between the two phases of Sensate Focus, Sensate Focus 1 and Sensate Focus 2.

The next and third chapter, *What Sensate Focus Is* Not: *A Little Bit of History About the Confusions*, includes a more conceptual perspective on the history of the confusions that have abounded about the purpose and implementation of Sensate Focus. However, it also contains what we consider to be invaluable, practical information on the actual words to use and avoid using when giving Sensate Focus instructions.

The remainder of this manual is primarily practical in nature. Nonetheless, it continually references the conceptual information contained in the first three chapters.

A Word About Citations

Since our goal was to write a reader-friendly, less academic manual, we have tried to limit the use of citations. People often find these distracting when trying to digest the substance of material. However, if you would like more detailed references we encourage you to turn to our earlier publications. These include Avery-Clark & Weiner (2017, in press), Linschoten, Weiner, & Avery-Clark (2016), Weiner & Avery-Clark (2014), and Weiner, Cannon, & Avery-Clark (2014). We hope you find *Sensate Focus in Sex Therapy: An Illustrated Manual* a valu-able resource, and we welcome your comments and contributions.

Chapter 2: Sensate Focus

William Masters and Virginia Johnson (1966; 1970) will be remembered for their landmark successes identifying and cataloging scientific data on human sexual response, and pioneering the first short-term treatment for sexual dysfunctions and distress. However, their most important contribution to the field of sex therapy may have been the creation and development of *Sensate Focus touching experiences* for identifying and resolving sexual difficulties and, ultimately, fostering and optimizing intimacy.

What is Sensate Focus?

The elegantly simple and straightforward technique of Sensate Focus is a radical departure from our cultural scripts about how sex happens. We are taught that to be a good lover you have to skillfully turn on your partner and your partner has to skillfully turn you on. Additionally, you have to do this by what amounts to reading your partner's mind and knowing what your partner will enjoy without your partner's having to share anything. All you have to do is look at the magazines at your local grocery store check-out line to learn *Ten Easy Steps for Turning on Your Boyfriend* or *How to Make Your Wife Horny*.

The way sex actually works is just the opposite. It is all about zeroing in on sensations for yourself in the moment and without expectations for any particular response. If you focus on sensations for yourself, sex will happen naturally. Sensate Focus teaches you how to do just that, how to reconnect to the sensory roots of sexuality when you have become lost.

Sensate Focus is a series of structured touching and discovery suggestions that provides opportunities for experiencing your own and your partner's bodies in a non-demand, exploratory way without having to read each other's minds. Non-demand exploration is defined as touching for your own interest without regard for trying to make sexual response, pleasure, enjoyment or relaxation happen for yourself or your partner, or prevent them from happening. Touching for your own interest is further defined as focusing on the touch sensations of temperature, pressure, and texture. Temperature, pressure, and texture are even more specifically defined as cool or warm, hard or soft (firm or light), and smooth or rough.

Sensate Focus works because arousal, pleasure, enjoyment, and relaxation are emotions, and emotions are physiologically-based *natural functions* that, by definition, *are not under direct voluntary control.* Trying to make them happen, or trying to prevent them from happening, is the single most common psychological cause of sexual dysfunction. Sensate Focus helps people learn to stop trying to directly control the natural function of sexual responsiveness in order to allow it to happen on its own. The Sensate Focus attitude of touching for interest gets your conscious mind out of the way, clearing the path for the body to respond naturally.

During Sensate Focus, when people focus on anything other than touch sensations, they are encouraged to treat these other thoughts and feelings as distractions, and to refocus on the dependable, touch sensations in a mindful way and as often as necessary. This is identical to mindfulness practice. It also involves the focusing principle of the cognitive and behavioral techniques of systematic desensitization and relaxation training, namely, that you cannot pay attention to two things at the same moment in time. Focusing on touching for your interest reduces performance anxiety (often caused by expectations to respond sexually) because you cannot zero in simultaneously on both tactile sensations and anxiety-producing thoughts.

Why is Sensate Focus Used?

Practitioners use Sensate Focus for many reasons. One is identifying the psychological, relationship, lifestyle, and sociocultural issues that contribute to sexual difficulties. Other reasons include teaching new skills to remediate sexual issues, and also eventually facilitating more satisfying and meaningful sexual intimacy.

Why is Sensate Focus Based on Touch?

Why touch sensations? "If words are the currency of poetry, and color is the currency of art, touch is the currency of sex" (Masters, Johnson, and Kolodny, 1995, p. 358). "The sense of touch is the special sense most used in sexual interchange" (Masters & Johnson, 1986, p. 8). In fact, what led to the development of Sensate Focus in the first place was Virginia Johnson's reflection on the memory of her mother's comforting "facial tracing" during her childhood (Maier, 2009, p. 182). She was not the first to recognize the power of touch.

> The *Upanishads*, one of the oldest spiritual texts,
> tell us that the energy that supports all creation manifests as
> the warmth that arises when we are touched.
>
> (Aanstoos, 2012, p. 51)

Over the centuries, literary masters have also reflected on the power of touch:

> See how she leans her cheek upon her hand.
> O, that I were a glove upon that hand
> That I might touch that cheek!
>
> (Shakespeare, *Romeo and Juliet*)

Philosophers suggest that skin-to-skin contact is the gateway to the "openness of the body … [to] our deepest relational intertwining with the flesh of the world" (Aanstoos, 2012, p. 57).

Sensate Focus

Scientific research suggests as much. Touch is the first sensation we experience before and immediately after birth. It often remains the most emotionally significant sense throughout our lives. It alters our biochemistry, our neurology, our feelings, thoughts, and behaviors, our ability to socialize and have intimate relationships, our ability to heal, thrive, and survive. In fact, touch may determine whether an infant lives or dies. Neurobiologists and psychiatrists have discovered that children whose senses are intact and who are provided with food and shelter but who do not receive and give touch suffer physically and psychologically. Researchers have shown that elderly people whose other senses are failing function better physically and psychologically when they can give and receive touch, and function much less well if they cannot (Konnikova, 2015). Helen Keller is a remarkable example of someone who, deprived of the sense of sight and hearing, was able to lead a healthy and deeply meaningful life in large measure because of the power of touch. It is this power that Masters and Johnson originally harnessed when they developed Sensate Focus.

> Use of the common denominator of sensory experience is employed in reversal of the presenting sexual distress … Communication intended to give comfort or solace, convey reassurance, show devotion, describe love or physical need is expressed first by touch. Olfactory, visual, or auditory communication generally serves as a reinforcement of the experience … Touch … becomes the primary medium of exchange …
>
> (Masters & Johnson, 1970, p. 66)

The purpose of Sensate Focus is and always has been to help sexually distressed individuals resolve their concerns by grounding them in touch sensations in the moment.

Why Does Focusing on Touch Sensations Help with Sexual Dysfunctions?
It is clear why touch is so powerful. But why would focusing on touch sensations help sexually distressed people with their problems? Three reasons.

Reliability and Tangibility
First, as clinicians, if we suggest to our clients that they stop focusing on their conscious anxiety about sexual responsiveness ("Will I get an erection?" "Will I be orgasmic?") we have to give them something else on which to focus instead. Turning your attention to sensations is a reliable, neutral, and tangible alternative to focusing on the worrisome thoughts and feelings that are often powerful contributors to sexual problems. Sensations give you something *dependable* on which to focus because sensations are always there. You cannot reliably get rid of performance thoughts and feelings about what has happened in the past, what may happen in the future, or what is or is not happening in the present moment. But you can always turn your attention to the tangible sensations of temperature, pressure, and texture.

The Gateway to Arousal
Second, it also happens that turning your attention to touch sensations is often the most powerful portal into sexual responsiveness. Focus on tactile sensations, get the conscious mind out of the way, and the body knows what to do. The benefits of this include decreased blood pressure, the release of oxytocin (the bonding hormone), and blood flow to the pelvis

that serves as the foundation of sexual interest and sexual arousal. Your conscious attention then moves *beyond being aware of even the sensations*, and you become absorbed in the flow of the sexual experience. This is the ultimate aim of Sensate Focus.

The Gateway to Relating Sexually

Finally, focusing on the touch sensations not only leads to your own arousal but also to your partner's. William Masters often said that the main sources of sexual stimulation are three-fold: your touching; your being touched; and your partner's arousal. Each person's arousal becomes part of an ongoing, positive feedback loop that serves as another gateway into the other person's arousal. *This loop moves the partners beyond merely self-focused touching into sexual relatedness and enhancement.*

The Main Concept Underlying Sensate Focus: Sex is a Natural Function

An understanding of the reliability and power of mindful touch leads into an understanding of the most important idea underlying Sensate Focus, namely, that sex is a natural function. This is central to appreciating how and why Sensate Focus works.

What is a Natural Function?

All natural functions have three characteristics in common.

We Are Born With Natural Functions

First, and barring major organic pathology, all natural functions are wired into us from before birth. This includes vegetative functions like breathing or digesting food, and emotional responses like pleasure, relaxation, and enjoyment. The same is true with sexual responsive-ness. We are born with the ability to respond sexually. Baby boys have erections *in utero*, and newborn girls are known to lubricate. Are these reactions all there is to sexuality? Obviously not. But they do suggest a natural, physiological readiness to respond in ways that are later considered sexual.

We Cannot Be Taught Natural Functions

Second, we do not have to be taught, nor can we be taught, these natural responses. While we can teach people to do things to increase the chances that these natural responses will occur (this is what therapists do all the time), we cannot *directly* teach the natural func-tions themselves. Just as the notion of instructing someone to sleep or to feel joyful seems nonsensical, similarly the notion that you can be taught to feel sexually desirous, have an erection, lubricate, or be orgasmic is preposterous. People can be encouraged to engage in doing things that increase the *likelihood* that the natural function of sexual responsiveness will occur (this is the essence of Sensate Focus), but even the most skilled practitioner cannot instill in a client the ability to respond sexually if the natural function is not wired in to begin with or if it is disrupted by medical or psychological problems or other factors.

We Do Not Have Direct Control Over Natural Functions

Finally, although we do have some ability to control our natural functions (you can hold your breath), we do not have the ability to intentionally make these functions happen or keep them from happening. For example, you can only hold your breath for so long. Another illustration involves producing a urine specimen when you visit the doctor. Have you noticed how the harder you try, the more difficult it becomes? Conscious demand to directly control a natural function creates anxiety, and anxiety interferes with the expression of any natural function.

The Paradox of Sexual Responsiveness

The same is true with sexual functioning. The paradox of sexual desire, arousal, and orgasm is that the harder you consciously try to make them happen, the less likely they are to happen, and the more intent you are on trying to keep them from happening, the more likely they are to happen. Conscious intentionality produces tremendous anxiety because you simply do not have direct, voluntary control over making yourself, or someone else, sexually aroused. The anxiety associated with trying to turn on yourself or your partner is at the heart of many non-medically based sexual dysfunctions and disorders. In a world in which most successful people have been rewarded for working hard for results, this paradox is very different from the usual manner in which we approach tasks.

The Formula for Implementing Sensate Focus Using Research-Based Techniques

Understanding and taking advantage of the concept and paradox of sex as a natural function, Masters and Johnson began helping people with sexual problems. They discovered that our romantic ideals of creating sexual responsiveness directly in ourselves and our partners, as well as the admonition we have received *not* to be self-focused in sexual encounters, are all wrong. What they realized through their laboratory and interview research is that people who are functioning well sexually practice three skills that honor sex as a paradoxical natural function: (1) while touching their partners, they *touch for themselves* rather than for their partners; (2) while touching or being touched, they focus on touching for their own *interest, curiosity, or exploration* (defined as focusing on tactile sensations) rather than for arousal, pleasure, relaxation, enjoyment, or any other emotion; and (3) they *redirect their attention* back to sensations when they are distracted. An understanding of the role of natural function and these three attitudinal skill sets are the foundation of Sensate Focus. Let's examine them in more detail.

Touching for Self vs. Touching for the Partner

Keeping the principle of sex as a natural function in mind, the first critical aspect of using Sensate Focus is the attitude of *touching for self.* The Masters and Johnson approach of touching for self was entirely new when it was developed. It put forth the radical idea that sexual responsiveness is essentially *self-focused.* This means that in order to become sexually responsive, you have to focus *mainly* on your own experience rather than on your partner's. This is different from being selfish where you are *only* focused on yourself. During Sensate Focus, the partner's experience is not ignored as will be described in more detail subsequently. The problem is that in our culture, we have been taught that being self-focused *is* the same as being selfish. However, in order for any natural function to express itself, a person must be absorbed in his or her own sensory experience. Everyone has to know how to tune into his or her own sensory experience in order to *allow* sexual responses to happen naturally. Let's put it this way: About whom are you thinking when you are orgasmic? You cannot be orgasmic and focused on your partner's experience at that same moment in time.

This is where focusing on the partner becomes a problem in the initial stages of Sensate Focus. It follows that if you cannot directly control natural functions for yourself, how are you going to make them happen or keep them from happening for someone else? We know this when it comes to other natural functions. Do you ever think that you can digest food for someone else? Or cry for them? Sexual responsiveness is no different. It requires a self-focused attitude. Touching for the partner generally doesn't work because you are out of your own experience. Not only that, but if the partner senses you are touching for them in order to turn them on, the pressure on the partner to respond sexually creates anxiety in them as well. This becomes a negative rather than a positive feedback loop for both participants.

Instead, Masters and Johnson suggested that what really happens in good sex is that each person becomes involved in touching for his or her own interest, using the partner's body as one source of absorption and stimulation in a mutually agreed upon lend lease proposition. This, then, creates a positive feedback loop that eventually is more likely to lead to arousal for both partners.

Touching for Interest by Focusing on Sensations vs. Touching for Pleasure or Arousal

The attitude of touching for yourself without judgments, expectations, and evaluations about arousal, pleasure, and the like is easier said than done. It is accomplished by the second critical attitude of Sensate Focus, *touching for interest* rather than for arousal or pleasure. Clients are encouraged to move away from judgments, expectations, and evaluations about arousal and pleasure because doing so leads to a demanding, performance-oriented mindset: "Am I doing a good job?" "Am I succeeding?" "Am I touching the right way?"

However, it is impossible *not* to attend to these judgments, expectations, and evaluations without *something else* on which to focus instead. Sensate Focus provides just this, a dependable alternative to anxious thoughts in the form of concrete, tangible, touch sensations in the here-and-now. These touch sensations are identified for clients as *temperature*, *pressure*, and *texture*, and even more concretely as *cool* or *warm*, *firm* (*hard*) or *light* (*soft*), and *smooth* or *rough* so that there is no confusion about what they may focus on instead of judgments, expectations, and evaluations.

Identifying and Managing Distractions

The third aspect of implementing Sensate Focus is identifying and managing distractions, especially those having to do with demands for the natural responses of arousal, pleasure, relaxation, and enjoyment. Clients are encouraged to identify anything other than temperature, texture, and pressure as a *distraction*. Distractions besides anxiety about performance may include thoughts about things left undone at home or at work, worrying about someone's knocking on the door, or negative feelings about yourself or your partner, among many others.

In the beginning of therapy, suggestions are extreme. Even positive thoughts like "I am having such a wonderful time" are treated as distractions in order to drive home the point that focusing on *anything* other than touch sensations is a distraction and is best managed by refocusing on the touch sensations. Again, this takes advantage of the main principle of the behavioral treatment techniques known as systematic desensitization and relaxation training, namely, that you cannot focus on distracting and anxiety-producing thoughts and experiences and, at the exact same time, attend to something else. In this case the something else is touch.

The Purpose of Sensate Focus: Mindfully Touching for Your Interest

The primary purpose of Sensate Focus can be summarized in this way: "Each partner touches *for self* and focuses on his or her own sensory experience *without regard for the partner's or one's own pleasure*" (Weiner & Avery-Clark, 2013). This is the same as what has come to be known as the practice of *mindfulness*. "Mindfulness practice is an ancient tradition in Eastern philosophy that forms the basis for meditation, and it is increasingly making its way into Western approaches to health care" (Brotto & Heiman, 2007, p. 3). Mindfulness is an attitude of here-and-now, self-focused awareness during which each sensation, emotion, intuition, thought, and feeling that captures your attention is acknowledged and accepted just as it is without judgment or evaluation.

We have been to conferences where, and read publications in which, Sensate Focus is described as *similar to* mindfulness practice. Our opinion is that Sensate Focus *is* mindfulness practice. Just as meditation, yoga, hypnosis, guided imagery, and deep breathing training aid clients with managing stress and debilitating moods by redirecting distractions and focusing on some type of sensory information, so Sensate Focus helps clients turn their attention from disconcerting experiences onto neutral, reliable tactile sensations. In the case of meditation, the sensory information may be auditory in the form of a mantra. In yoga it is kinesthetic in the form of physical sensations in different positions. In hypnosis it may be visual stimuli on which your eyes focus either outside of yourself or inside your head. In the case of guided imagery it may also be visual imagery. With deep breathing training it is the auditory sound and kinesthetic feel of your body inhaling and exhaling. In the case of Sensate Focus, it is the sensations of touch. All of these increase the likelihood that future-oriented anxiety will lessen and a desired natural response in the present will be more likely to happen.

The Difference Between Sensate Focus 1 and Sensate Focus 2

Although we have been using the general term *Sensate Focus* to identify the hierarchical touching suggestions, we make a distinction between two phases of Sensate Focus, as we have suggested. What we have been describing thus far is more accurately referred to as *Sensate Focus 1*. However, there is also another phase that we call *Sensate Focus 2*. This is because just as there is more to sex than natural responses, so there is more to Sensate Focus than touching for your interest.

While we will be discussing Sensate Focus 2 in more detail at the end of this manual, we are emphasizing the components of Sensate Focus 1 in order to underscore the importance of mastering sex as a natural function, and mastering its attitudinal and practical applications of touching for your own interest, *before* moving on to Sensate Focus 2. Sensate Focus 1 involves mastering skills for people who are having sexual difficulties. Sensate Focus 2 is for people who are not having difficulties, or who have resolved their difficulties, and who want to enhance sexual satisfaction. The difference between Sensate Focus 1 and Sensate Focus 2 is similar to the difference between a child who is under the age of two years and one who is over the age of two. The reason the first two years of life are often referred to as the *sensori-motor* period is that children must learn how to take in sensory experience and navigate around their small worlds before they can form concepts from these sensations and move on to learning how to relate to others according to complex social guidelines, all of which represents the *operational* years of development. In the case of Sensate Focus, formal sexual dysfunctions need to be resolved first in Sensate Focus 1 before clients can move on to that for which many people really come to sex therapy, namely, cultivating more sexually relational and optimal experiences that are romantic, pleasurable, arousing, relaxing, and even transcendent. This is Sensate Focus 2.

Chapter 3: What Sensate Focus is *Not*: A Little Bit of History About the Confusions

Sensate Focus seems pretty straightforward, doesn't it? Unfortunately, that hasn't always been the case. This next chapter covers a bit of the history of Sensate Focus in order to clarify the confusions about how Sensate Focus is understood and implemented. If you are not a history buff, you can move to the next chapter without missing much of the practical information. However, this history clarifies why we spend so much time emphasizing the critical importance of both appreciating sex as a natural function and also the attitude of touching for your own interest when it comes to using Sensate Focus effectively. The history also indicates the power of the words that are chosen for Sensate Focus suggestions, and these words may hinder or facilitate therapeutic progress.

Almost from the moment *Human Sexual Inadequacy* (Masters & Johnson, 1970) was published, there was confusion about what Sensate Focus was all about and how to use it. Even as talented clinicians training under Masters and Johnson enlarged the sex therapy field from its original and medically based, psycho-educational model, the original purpose of Sensate Focus was either poorly communicated in their publications or never published at all. Masters and Johnson were aware of their role in these misunderstandings, and they acknowledged that *Human Sexual Inadequacy* does not accurately portray the intention of Sensate Focus.

Confusion About the Concept of Sex as a Natural Function
The confusion about the main idea underlying Sensate Focus, that sex is a natural function, has to do not so much with the concept itself but more with a lack of appreciation for its profound significance. We don't know of one sex therapist who wouldn't agree with the notion that sexual responsiveness is something with which we are all born, that we cannot be taught, and that is under some limited but not direct voluntary control. And most people who are not even sex therapists would also nod heads in agreement.

But do any of us really live sex as a natural function? While we know that we do not have direct, ongoing control over other natural functions like sleep, food digestion, or our emotions, we live in a culture that treats sexual responsiveness as something different, as if it were under our direct control.

Another confusion has to do with recognizing the meaning of sex as a natural function. Some sexologists have suggested that viewing sex as a natural function is an inaccurate oversimplification of sex, one that is based only on biology (Tiefer, 1991). The first sexologists who would agree that there is more to sex than biology would be Masters and Johnson themselves. They clearly recognized that sex is more than anatomy, biochemistry, physiology, neurology, and endocrinology. Their emphasis on sex as a natural function does not exclude psychological, interpersonal, social, and even spiritual dimensions. However, by emphasizing sex as a natural, psychophysiological process, Masters and Johnson were reminding us that it is all too easy to forget that the natural processes of sexuality are its bedrock, and that it is often necessary to focus on this physical bedrock _before_ attending to other factors when treating sexual dysfunctions. This is true not only in sex therapy but also in life in general. The famous psychologist Abraham Maslow (1954) suggests exactly this same principle in his well-known _hierarchy of needs_ when he stresses that the basic physiological needs must be met before all others can be pursued.

Confusions About Sensate Focus Suggestions: The Importance of Touch for Mindful Self-Focus

Confusion about the full conceptual measure of sex as a natural function has often translated into misunderstandings about the words that are used to convey Sensate Focus instructions. This is particularly true for initial Sensate Focus suggestions.

Some would contend that the words we use are not particularly significant and that to quibble over them is to play semantics. Others suggest that words are at best inadequate: "The human tongue is like a cracked cauldron on which we beat out tunes to set a bear dancing when we would make the stars weep with our melodies" (Flaubert, 1965, p. 138). We are going to suggest that, at least for the purposes of accurately conveying and processing the concepts and suggestions associated with Sensate Focus 1, _the words therapists and clients choose are of paramount importance_. Words have the power to convey attitudes that help the clients moderate pressure, or attitudes that can add to the pressure. Much as cognitive-behavior therapy practitioners advise, the verbal narratives we tell ourselves make all the difference in the world in terms of: our emotions; our ability to cope with disruptive ones by cultivating productive attitudes; and our ability to translate these into more effective behavior patterns (Ellis, 2000).

The confusions over the concept of sex as a natural function, and the practical Sensate Focus suggestions that come out of this concept, are perfect examples of the power of language to shape emotions, attitudes, and even behavior. They began with Masters and Johnson's own and unfortunate choice of words when initially describing Sensate Focus. Masters and Johnson seem to have accurately conveyed the idea that sexual responsivity could not be produced on demand. They did this by avoiding using phrases like _make yourself sexually aroused_ when offering the Sensate Focus instructions. However, they did use words that implied a demand for other natural, emotional responses, most notably, _pleasure._ They also used language that emphasized creating these natural responses _for the partner._

> The partner who is pleasuring is committed first to do just that: give pleasure. At a second level in the experience, the giver is to explore his or her own … personal pleasure in doing the touching to experience and appreciate … the somewhat indescribable aura of physical receptivity expressed by the partner being pleasured. After a reasonable time … the … partners are to exchange roles of pleasuring (giving) and being pleasured (getting).
>
> (Masters & Johnson, 1970, p. 68)

It is this *emphasis on producing pleasure*, especially the *partner's pleasure*, that resulted in major confusion when it comes to implementing Sensate Focus suggestions. Apfelbaum (2012) correctly describes how, as a result, many professionals have interpreted the first phase of Sensate Focus as *non-demand pleasuring of the partner*.

Thus, understandably, the purpose of Sensate Focus often has been presented in the professional literature as emphasizing the goals of creating enjoyable, relaxing, romantic, or pleasurable emotions particularly for the partner but even for oneself. Inadvertently, this wording pressures clients to make these emotions happen for each other and for themselves. This is not only a double whammy but also the incorrect use of Sensate Focus that may have negative therapeutic consequences. In fact, clinicians lament, "In clinical supervision, we often hear reports that therapeutic disasters resulted from incorrect usage of sensate focus" (Weeks & Gambescia, 2009, p. 360). One of the most common forms of incorrect use is incorrect wording. This is also one of the most significant contributors to resistance on the part of clients to participate in Sensate Focus.

The Problem with Using "Touching for Pleasure" Words

All of this suggests the need for clinicians to be careful when choosing the words for initial Sensate Focus directions. Directions that incorporate phrases like "focus on sensations" and "pay attention to temperature, pressure, and texture" are much more therapeutic than ones like "give pleasure," "try to relax," or "enjoy being touched."

The word "feeling" should be avoided. Clinicians will say, "Pay attention to what you are feeling." Since people often think of "feeling" as synonymous with the words "emotion" and "sensation," it is better to stay away from this word altogether. If clients interpret "feeling" as meaning "emotion," they are likely to pressure themselves to experience arousal, pleasure, or relaxation, experiences they cannot make happen. This is counterproductive to the therapeutic goals of non-demand touching for self-focused interest.

Other tricky words are "sensual" and "sensuality." Our suggestion is that clinicians avoid using these words because clients are likely to interpret them as meaning "sexual" and they may, therefore, pressure themselves to become aroused. This is one of the reasons we stress using the word "sensation" in this manual. Focusing on sensations is quite a different experience from sensuality and sexuality, both of which have a more goal-oriented connotation. Even the word "sensation" requires clear definition as "temperature, pressure, and texture."

The Problem with Using "Touching for Partner" Words

Using phrases that encourage clients to *pleasure the partner* puts them in a doubly pressuring situation to produce not just their own natural response but also a natural response for someone else. It is helpful to avoid words like "giving" or "receiving," or identifying the person touching as "the giver" and the person being touched as the "receiver." This is why we will refer to the partners as "the Toucher" and "the Touchee." Words like "massage" or "back rub" can also trigger clients to fall back into a partner-oriented approach to touching and should be avoided.

The Ramifications of, and Resolutions to, the Confusions

It is unclear why Masters and Johnson's original Sensate Focus suggestions were not consistent with the notion of natural functions. Perhaps Masters and Johnson did not appreciate the importance of the words they used (phrases like "touching for *pleasure*" as opposed to "touching for *interest*," "attend to what you are *feeling*" rather than "focus on *sensations*"). Perhaps they did not appreciate the effect these words would have on the interpretation of Sensate Focus instructions by future clinicians. Perhaps they actually changed their suggestions once they understood how counter their original instructions were to the approach they hoped to convey.

The good news is that by the 1983 training program in which we participated, Masters and Johnson had changed the wording of the instructions. On February 21, 1983, during the Sensate Focus component of the post-doctoral training program in sex therapy at the Masters & Johnson Institute (that initiated our five years of clinical and research work at the Institute), Robert Kolodny, Masters and Johnson's associate and third author on many publications, outlined the following:

Purpose of Sensate Focus/Process of Sensate Focus

- to get in touch with senses
- to reduce spectatoring → goal orientation – i.e., to get at neutrality …
- to get at self-representation and responsibility
- to get at the neutrality – staying in here-and-now

(Avery-Clark, 1983, p. 1)

Throughout the 1983 postgraduate training at the Institute, the aims of Sensate Focus were clearly delineated as "the toucher is to touch for themselves [*sic*] – trace … with intention of taking in sensations. Don't evaluate – just experience – stay in neutrality," and "Encourage exploration, experimentation," "Touching for self – focus on your partner's body for your own self, own interest, what's going on with you – not a massage to please them, not a turn on to please them," and "Touching for Self … It's not something you do – it's an attitude." It is evident that Sensate Focus was, by that point, described in sensory-oriented, non-demand, *touching for your interest* terms, terms that we believe may be more conducive to therapeutic progress.

Chapter 4: Sexual Dysfunctions: Basic Issues, Assessment Procedures, and Collaborative Treatment Planning

What is Sexual Dysfunction, and How Does it Differ from Occasional Sexual Difficulty?

Occasional sexual difficulties are universal and most people will experience them temporarily and intermittently in the course of their normal sexual lives. These include: lack of sexual interest or desire; problems with erection or arousal; rapid, delayed or absent orgasm; and sexual pain. If these occur every now and then, they are usually the result of a situational problem, like consuming too much alcohol. Most people shake them off with little problem.

Sexual dysfunctions, on the other hand, are longer lasting, occur more often, and result in much more emotional and relationship distress. They meet specific criteria as described in the recently published *DSM-5* (2015) that include occurring 75–100% of the time and having a duration of at least six months.

What Are the Causes of Sexual Dysfunctions?

Sexual dysfunctions can be caused by a number of factors. Although we will be emphasizing the psychosocial, it is important to consider the biomedical variables at the beginning of the therapy evaluation. Masters and Johnson emphasized the psychological, relationship, lifestyle, and cultural nature of what they believed to be the cause of the majority of sexual dysfunctions. However, they also said, "There is never any excuse for treating a physiological dysfunction as a psychological inadequacy" (Masters & Johnson, 1970, p. 53). It is extremely important, while identifying the factors that contribute to sexual dysfunctions, not to fall victim to *either/or* thinking. *Both/and* analysis is critical. Sometimes, as therapy and Sensate Focus progress, a sexual dysfunction that at first seemed to be caused by something medical (e.g., erection difficulty associated with a spinal cord injury) begins to improve. The body responds to Sensate Focus in spite of the medical problem as underlying psychological, relationship, and other sociocultural factors are addressed.

Sometimes it is not possible to identify the main issues involved in a sexual dysfunction during the early phases of assessment. It is important to keep an open mind, reminding clients that Sensate Focus is not only helpful for treating the sexual problem but also for determining what is contributing to or maintaining it. As Sensate Focus continues, factors that were not apparent at the beginning become more obvious.

Sometimes a *reported* sexual dysfunction is not the problem in need of treatment. For example, erection disorders may actually hide a problem with rapid ejaculation. Sometimes the presenting sexual dysfunction is not a dysfunction at all. A couple may bemoan a desire disorder when the partners are actually experiencing differences in their preferences for the frequency of sexual activity, neither of which falls under clinically diagnosable conditions.

Here are five of the most important areas to consider when looking at sexual dysfunctions.

Medical Factors

Since the concept of sex as a natural function points to the importance of underlying biomedical processes, it is logical to initiate assessment by looking for biomedical factors. These may include any condition or medication that affects endocrine (hormonal), cardiovascular (blood flow) or neurological (nerve conduction) functioning in the pelvic region. These conditions may be the result of: chronic illnesses (e.g., diabetes, hypothyroidism); prescribed, non-prescribed medications or "street" drugs; and/or medical interventions (e.g., radiation or prostate surgery).

Individual Factors

Individual issues include the client's overall psychological functioning (e.g., anxiety, mood disorders, trauma) as well as negative views of self, body, or sex. It is important to take a look at the client's distracting thoughts and feelings, especially those having to do with the sexual concern. Examining the client's sexual experience, techniques, preferences, awareness of these preferences, and knowledge about sexuality in general is also important. Historical issues include childhood neglect or abuse, and differing attachment styles (such as anxious or avoidant patterns).

Partner and Relationship Factors

It is always important to consider the partner's possible impact when looking at clients' sexual dysfunctions. These include the partner's illnesses, sexual dysfunctions, performance expectations, and responses to the sexual problems. Evaluating the partners' psychological functioning, and the partner's willingness to participate in therapy is vital. Understanding the partner's subjective experiences of his or her own sexual and relationship history, and the meaning placed on the presenting sexual dysfunctions, are also imperative.

Relationship distress may add to sexual dysfunctions. Conversely, relationship problems can be the result of sexual dysfunctions. Feelings of rejection, frustration, and inadequacy can lead to less positive feelings about partners, less frequent shows of affection, unhelpful or absent communication, and less quality time spent together. All of these may contribute to lowered satisfaction with intimacy in general and sexual intimacy in particular. Dealing with communication problems, power struggles, and unresolved conflicts and resentments in the relationship may not resolve the sexual concerns. However, failure to deal with them certainly won't resolve the sexual concerns. Addressing relationship issues is essential for laying the foundation for working on the sexual dysfunction.

Lifestyle Stressors

A topic that is sometimes overlooked in the evaluation of sexual dysfunctions is the effect of other demands on the individual's or couple's time. What are the professional or job responsibilities? How stressful are these? What about the impact of children, relatives, and others? Is involvement with parents an issue? The main purpose of looking at these is to clarify the amount and quality of time the partners have to devote to themselves and to their relationship. Other stressors may include: job or personal losses; lack of exercise; overeating; and habits that contribute negatively to the client's overall physical and psychological health.

Sociocultural Influences

It is essential to review the effect that family of origin, social, and religious factors have on sexual functioning. Although most clinicians assess the impact of these variables on women in terms of their constraining effects, and on men in terms of their pressuring effects, it is so important not to presume that the opposites aren't also significant factors. Taking a look at the extent and nature of the sexual values, scripts, and misinformation affecting each partner is necessary.

Mixed or Unknown Etiology

All of this suggests that there are a number of factors contributing to a sexual dysfunction including a new area of interest – environmental toxins (Reddy, 2016). However, the exact causes may be unclear even by the end of the evaluation. Interestingly enough and quite often, clients progress regardless of whether all the original etiological factors have been identified. Sometimes the clinician needs to initiate therapy to determine what is actually causing the problem. As noted, Sensate Focus is useful for teasing out these variables.

An example of this might be the low desire client who reports no obvious causes of the sudden loss of interest. Even the results of the medical evaluation may be negative. It is often helpful to begin Sensate Focus to identify the contributing causes of the dysfunction. Usually by the time the couple has moved to Sensate Focus with *breasts, chests, and genitals on limits* (described later on), the most significant individual and couple issues contributing to the sexual dysfunction become apparent.

Another example is when a woman who reports taking a medication for anxiety due to stress at work has her first reported difficulty with orgasm. The partner responds in a strong, negative way. This only adds to the woman's orgasmic concerns when the couple approaches the next sexual encounter. Then the woman has more difficulty being orgasmic. It is not too long before this pattern is established. What might have begun as a stressful work and medication-related difficulty becomes a much larger, psychological and relationship problem leading to dysfunction.

How Are Sexual Dysfunctions Evaluated and Treated?

Sex therapy begins with a thorough assessment of these medical, psychological, relational, cultural, and lifestyle factors that might impact sexual functioning. Here are some ways to do this.

Medical Examination

A thorough medical examination by a primary physician or a sexual medicine specialist (e.g., endocrinologist, pelvic floor specialist, trained gynecologist or urologist) is often recommended to add to the interview process and treatment itself. Understanding the interaction between medical and psychosocial factors requires looking at medicines, hormones, and health issues in addition to doing therapy. Although we are leaving an analysis of biomedical factors in sexual dysfunctions to other sexological experts, we do not want to ignore the need for their assessment as part of a thorough evaluation and treatment program.

Taking the History

Most sex therapy evaluations begin with, and are devoted primarily to, taking a formal, detailed, self- and partner-report history (Althof, Rubio-Aurioles, & Perelman, 2012). Appendix A is a sample sexual history interview form that may be helpful. If the clinician is following Masters and Johnson's original protocol, the evaluation usually begins with both partners being seen together to review past and present therapy and current therapy goals. It includes examining the relationship dynamics, individual strengths, and motivation of both partners.

The initial couple's session is followed by the individual psychosocial evaluation, referred to as *history-taking*. This involves between one and three sessions for each partner. Additional history-taking sessions can be included as needed.

The focus during the history-taking is on individual psychological concerns such as identifying anxiety, depression, psychosis, substance abuse, trauma, and beliefs about any physical challenges. These problems make short-term therapy difficult and may indicate the need for medications or other types of treatments. Other important issues include attachment styles, family of origin, relationship and sexual history, and the partners' perceptions of one another and of the presenting problem(s). The history-taking

> is structured to develop material within a chronologic framework of life-cycle influences, which reflects sexually oriented attitudes and feelings, expectations and experiences, environmental changes and practices. History-taking certainly must provide information sufficient to define the character (etiological background, symptom onset, severity and duration, psychosocial affect) of the presenting sexual dysfunctions. Equally important, history-taking contributes knowledge of the basic personalities of the ... partners and develops a professional concept of their interpersonal relationship adequate to determining (1) changes that may be considered desirable, (2) personal resources and the depth and health of the psychosocial potential from which they can be drawn, and (3) [relationship]-unit motivation and goals (what the ... partners actually expect from therapy).
>
> (Masters & Johnson, 1970, p. 24)

The most important aspect of the individual history-taking is what is referred to as *phenomenological* evaluation, or what Masters and Johnson referred to as an assessment of the clients' *sexual value system.* It is important for clinicians to understand how clients *actually experience* within themselves and within their psychosocial situation whatever they are describing. They need to understand how clients subjectively experience their sexuality, dysfunction, sexual relationship, and sexual background. What does the problem *mean* to them? What value do they put on the problem? How do they feel about it? What emotions are triggered by the problem? What thoughts do they have about it? The emphasis is not so much on what *actually* or "*factually*" has happened or is happening outside of themselves. It is not about passing judgment on the experience as good or bad, right or wrong. The emphasis is, quite simply, on how whatever happened or is happening comes across to each client, how the client takes in and processes the experiences. An understanding of this sexual value system is critical for making sure that the treatment is sensitive to each client's core sexual values and experiences.

Sexual Dysfunctions

The most helpful attitude clinicians may adopt during the individual history-taking is one of treating "the individual as a whole person ... When taken out of context of the total being and his environment, a 'sex' history per se would be as relatively meaningless as a 'heart' history or a 'stomach' history" (Masters & Johnson, 1970, p. 23). Out of the psychosocial sexual history emerges each client's sexual value system, "derived from sensory experiences individually invested with erotic meaning" and "reinforced by years of psychosocial adaptation" (Masters & Johnson, 1970, pp. 24–25).

Inventories

Some clinicians add intake surveys to this formal history. To gather information on female desire, arousal, and orgasm dysfunctions, Cynthia Graham (Graham, 2010) and Lori Brotto and her research team (Brotto et al., 2010) suggest using the following inventories: Golombok-Rust Inventory of Sexual Satisfaction (GRISS); Brief Index of Sexual Functioning for Women (BISF-W); Sexual Desire Inventory (SDI); Derogatis Interview for Sexual Functioning (DISF); Female Sexual Function Index (FSFI); Sexual Function Questionnaire (SFQ); Female Sexual Distress Scale (FSDS); Sexual Interest and Desire Inventory (SIDI); Hypoactive Sexual Desire Disorder (HSDD) Screener; Female Sexual Distress Scale-Revised (FSDS-R); and Women's Sexual Interest Diagnostic Interview (WSID).

Collecting information on sexual desire, erectile dysfunction, and orgasmic concerns in men, including *hidden* variables, can be simplified by using the International Index of Erectile Function (IIEF) and the Male Sexual Health Questionnaire (MSHQ) as well as the GRISS and FSFI (Meana & Steiner, 2014; Perelman, 2014; Rosen, Miner, & Wincze, 2010).

The Roundtable Session

Once the history-taking and inventory use have been completed, clients are invited to a *roundtable* session. There are three main aspects to the roundtable.

Treatment Planning

During the roundtable session, therapists share their understanding of the etiological and maintenance factors contributing to their sexual and relational difficulties, and suggest the treatment plan for these concerns. This is done together with the clients' feedback as the planning and implementation of sex therapy and Sensate Focus is always an ongoing and joint effort between participants and therapists.

Although understanding the couple's full individual and relationship history and current concerns underscored their work, the focus of Masters and Johnson's original, intensive Sensate Focus approach emphasized only those factors that had immediate impact on the sexual problem. The goal of sex therapy and Sensate Focus is *to do as much but no more than necessary* to resolve the concern.

As a result of the history-taking sessions and other evaluative techniques, therapists and clients work together to create the therapeutic format. Here are some questions to consider:

Will Sensate Focus be Used Together With, Before, or After Medical Treatment?
Many clients seek out medical interventions such as medications, surgeries, physical therapy, and other medical resources before seeing a sex therapist. They come to therapy when these solutions have not worked or when partners come to agreement that they prefer non-medical

interventions first, or in combination with medications. As sex therapists, we believe in listening to the client's values while advising them of their options. We believe in utilizing a collaborative approach that involves medical intervention along with sex therapy in most cases.

Will Therapy be Short Term and Intensive or Longer Term and More In-Depth?

Short-term, intensive therapy (for example, having therapy sessions more than one time a week) works best if clients have a difficult time carving out time for their relationship at home, if one or both partners travel a lot for work, if the relationship is in severe crisis, or if they live some distance from the therapist's office. The advantage of the short-term, intensive approach is that results are usually experienced more quickly. However, longer-term, weekly, or bi-weekly treatment is more practical for most clients and clinicians. The advantage of the less frequent, longer-term program is that the skills learned in therapy are already being worked into the clients' regular lives while they are engaged in sex and relationship therapy. Intensive, short-term treatment usually has to be combined with a re-entry period during which clients have to address working their skills into their daily routines. However, this can usually be handled with later booster sessions when the clients revisit skills learned during the intensive treatment program.

Will Therapy Include One or Both Partners?

"Treatment is sometimes divided into two phases: treatment when there is no partner and later resumption of treatment when [clients] establish a new relationship" (Althof, 2014, p. 125). Individual sex therapy and Sensate Focus is appropriate when there is no partner or when the partner is either unwilling or unable to come to the therapist's office. It can also help when there is an element of the sexual dysfunction that is best suited to individual intervention (e.g., in the case of Vaginismus where self-Sensate Focus and initial insertion of dilators may best be handled individually).

In general, it is difficult to use Sensate Focus effectively unless both partners participate in therapy at least at some point. Obviously, it is impossible to use the Sensate Focus couples techniques without having both partners. However, perhaps the most important reason to consider including both partners in sex therapy and Sensate Focus has to do with Masters and Johnson's revolutionary treatment idea that it is not so much either partner that represents the client in therapy as it is the *relationship that is the client*. Regardless of which partner presents as the *identified client*, both are affected by the sexual difficulty and each is critical to resolving it.

Some clinicians have suggested that Masters and Johnson focused on the symptomatic partner rather than on the couple's relationship. This is difficult to understand in light of their description of sex therapy and Sensate Focus. In fact, they stressed that failure to include both partners is to ignore "half the problem" (Masters & Johnson, 1970, p. 3).

> There is no such thing as an uninvolved partner in any [relationship] in which there is some form of sexual inadequacy ... Isolating [either of the partners] in therapy from his or her partner not only denies the concept that both partners are involved in the sexual inadequacy with which their ... relationship is contending, but also ignores the fundamental fact that sexual response represents (either symbolically or in reality) interaction between people.
>
> (Masters & Johnson, 1970, p. 2)

Sexual Dysfunctions

Do One or Both Partners Need Individual Therapy for Another Issue Before or
During Sex Therapy?

Sometimes one or both partners may come to therapy with significant sexual or psychological issues that require individual sessions or separate individual therapy either before or during the implementation of sex therapy and Sensate Focus. This is most appropriate when one or both partners experience a serious problem that might interfere with Sensate Focus if it is not addressed. These conditions include clinical depression, bipolar disorder, psychosis, substance abuse, severe personality disorders, and/or a history of trauma or neglect, among others. Individual therapy may be recommended for partners who are in chaotic or toxic relationships.

However, Sensate Focus itself is such a powerful diagnostic and therapeutic technique that its very implementation may not only reveal psychological concerns of which clients may be unaware but also may have a stabilizing and progressive effect on the issues the individual and couple are experiencing. This means that not everything has to be entirely copasetic with either the individual partners or with the relationship before Sensate Focus is initiated. Sensate Focus may even serve as a useful technique for helping individuals and couples with non-sexual problems.

Should Clients Engage in Relationship Therapy?

Couples often ask whether or not they should have separate conjoint or relationship therapy before or during sex therapy. Even within the field, there is contention about the juxtaposition of relationship and sex therapy. In fact, sex therapy actually is, to a large extent, couples therapy. We are aware of the interactional nature of sexual and relationship issues. Whether the presenting problem began with relationship or sexual problems, both aspects of the couple's interaction are inevitably involved. In addition, many clients come to sex therapists after a successful couples therapy experience that has improved the relationship but not solved the sexual problem.

Will a Dual-Sex Therapist Team Be Involved or One Therapist?

Masters and Johnson famously invented the use of dual-sex therapy teams. However, this practice has fallen out of favor for a variety of reasons. Dual therapist teams may often help tremendously with sex therapy and Sensate Focus particularly if one or both partners have a preference for this approach or have a history that requires the development of a particularly strong transference with a same- or opposite-sex therapist. However, in most outpatient settings, a dual therapy team may not be available or practical. In our experience, if clients are encouraged to verbalize any discomfort or bias they experience with the single therapist approach, the Sensate Focus process usually moves along smoothly with only one clinician involved.

Important Attitudes and Skills

Once the format has been determined, several crucial attitudes are often introduced in this roundtable meeting. Without these, it is difficult to move forward in the initial phase of sex therapy and Sensate Focus.

Here-and-Now Mindfulness

The first of these attitudes is a clinical, neutral, Gestalt-like, mindful *here-and-now* approach both inside and outside the bedroom. This focuses on the present and as little as possible on the past ("This never worked before!") or future ("Will this work?"). The reason for this? Simple: No one can do anything about what has happened in the past or is going to happen in the future. The focus is on what can be in the now.

Radical Self-Responsibility

The other critical attitude introduced during the roundtable session is *radical self-responsibility*. It is identical to the attitude suggested by the Dalai Lama: "Do not let the behavior of others destroy your inner peace." This reinforces the idea that no matter what is going on with the partner, clients are responsible for managing their responses and following through with the suggestions. "Gradually, the partners comprehend their role in creating barriers to intimacy rather than focusing on a symptomatic partner" (Weeks & Gambescia, 2009, p. 342). It also helps clients to focus on their own experience of the touch rather than on what they think is going on with the partner. Too often clients, like all of us human beings, are likely to focus on what the other person is doing or not doing. In the case of Sensate Focus, this results in not following through with the touching sessions "because my partner didn't initiate when it was her turn," "because my partner didn't seem to be in the mood," "because my partner didn't move my hand away," "because my partner didn't seem to be focusing on sensations," or "because my partner said he wanted to do something else during the session." Not only does an attitude of radical self-responsibility diffuse projections of blame and get around unproductive interactions between the partners, but it also helps clients focus on that over which they have control (their own thoughts and behavior) and reinforces the first attitude above of here-and-now mindfulness.

Other Self-Management and Relationship Skills

In addition to the introduction of mindful and self-responsible attitudes, other self-management and relationship skills may be offered as needed. These include: communication skills; identifying, accepting, and managing feelings; negotiating differences; creative problem-solving; quality couple time; and using the partner as a resource. These are necessary to create, revive, and/or sustain a secure relational environment conducive to change.

Introducing Sensate Focus

The most important feature of the roundtable session for the purposes of this manual is the introduction of Sensate Focus 1. This is the subject of the next chapter. Not only is this the therapeutic centerpiece and primary modality through which sexual difficulties are more fully understood and addressed, it is also one of the aspects of the Masters and Johnson approach that has most influenced the field of sex therapy. It is a powerful way to move the didactic information offered during the therapy session out of the office and into the experiential context of the couple's bedroom. This, after all, is the purpose of sex therapy.

Chapter 5: Sensate Focus 1: The Non-Demand Touching Suggestions

Preliminaries

Before clients begin practicing Sensate Focus, there are some preliminary suggestions that make it less likely that there will be distractions, and that make it more likely that the touching sessions will go well. By going well we do not mean that there will be no problems. What we mean is that the problems that arise can be framed positively as being exactly the reasons for which clients have come to therapy, and as providing the opportunity to offer an intervention, a suggestion, or a skill. These preliminary suggestions are outlined in Appendix B and described in detail below.

Environment, Comfort, and Privacy

Couples are encouraged to have their touching sessions in any way that makes them feel as safe and comfortable as possible. For instance, it is usually helpful for them to be in a private, quiet setting with some lighting, a comfortable temperature, and as few external distractions as possible. For some couples, the bedroom is the best place while for others it is associated with too many negative experiences. Removing common interferences is important. These may include pets, children, telephones, television, music, and any other potential distractions. Locking the door may seem intuitive to therapists but this is not necessarily the case with clients.

Time and Atmosphere

Clients are encouraged to set aside some unpressured time together before the touching sessions begin. This is best done when clients are alert, and not right before they go to sleep or have just finished a large meal.

They begin the touching sessions with the clinical, here-and-now, self-responsible attitudes described previously, not with any expectations of sexual desire, arousal, or any other emotion. In fact, looking forward to the touching session, or experiencing any particular emotion like excitement or eager anticipation, *is not required* to initiate and participate in a touching session. In order to take away the pressure that arises from demands for specific emotions or arousal, the clients are discouraged, during both this pre-session time and the Sensate Focus opportunities themselves, from trying to cultivate a *romantic* or *relaxing* atmosphere. Participants, and often therapists as well, think that incorporating candles, music, or other supposedly romantic accessories into Sensate Focus will help it go more smoothly. However, attempting to create this type of atmosphere may be experienced as an unspoken demand for specific emotions like arousal, pleasure, relaxation, and enjoyment.

For the touching sessions themselves, clients are asked to have uninterrupted blocks of time during which they have a reasonably good chance of not being disturbed. If therapy is done intensively, clients may be asked to schedule as many as one or two touching opportunities daily. In a once-a-week outpatient setting, this is often changed to include something like two or three touching sessions a week.

Participants are initially encouraged to allow the sessions to happen spontaneously but no less often than every 48–72 hours. This is to make sure that sessions are taking place often enough to keep the physiological pot simmering on the back burner, so to speak. If the clients are having difficulty with this spontaneous approach, they are encouraged to formally schedule the touching sessions in the same way they would schedule any other appointment during the week. This often creates an opportunity for the therapist to discuss spontaneity being unreliable as a basis for creativity and sustaining intimacy in the early phases of Sensate Focus, and in long-term relationships in general. Much like having a dinner party, if you do not schedule the event and prepare for it, it is unlikely to take place. However, this does not mean that spontaneity will not take place during the event itself.

During the Sensate Focus sessions, the person touching is encouraged to touch long enough to get over any initial discomfort, and long enough to practice returning the focus of attention back to temperature, pressure, and texture, but not so long as to get tired or bored. The initial sessions often last between five and 15 minutes for each partner, but clients are discouraged from watching the clock or basing their length of touching on how long the partner touched. A shorter session during which they actively focus on the touch sensations, and return their attention to these sensations when distracted, is more helpful than a longer session during which they allow their minds to drift, especially to what is going on with their partners.

Initiation

It is often the client with the apparently presenting dysfunction who is encouraged to initiate the first Sensate Focus session. This relieves partner pressure to initiate and also may help with the partner's feelings of rejection based on prior history of unsuccessful initiation. The other partner initiates the second touching session, and from then on they may alternate. However, the initiation varies according to client personality, relationship dynamics, and cultural scripts. If one partner is especially apprehensive, he or she may initiate all of the sessions for a while, or might request that the other person do so. As with all aspects of Sensate Focus, this is open to collaborative planning between therapists and clients, and incorporates clients' feedback.

When initiating, participants are encouraged to do so by formally saying something like, "I would like to do the touching session now." This formality decreases the likelihood of one partner's failing to accurately interpret any informal cues from the initiator to begin the session. It also elicits anxious thoughts and emotions associated with the sessions because there is nothing like formally declaring that the touching session is going to happen to trigger the very roadblocks to sexual functioning for which the clients are seeking therapy. Thus, the formal initiation of sessions can be diagnostic as well as therapeutic.

Communication

Because most couples approach the initial Sensate Focus sessions with some degree of apprehension, it is not at all uncommon for them to talk nervously and to giggle during the initial touching. This is normalized, but they are urged to talk about their anxieties, only *before* and *after* the sessions and in the therapist's office. *During* the sessions they are invited to practice internal, mindful focus in order to minimize distractions caused by sounds and the content of what they may say. For example, the therapist may suggest something like this:

> It is very understandable that you might find yourself talking or chuckling during these early sessions because you feel uncomfortable. However, one of the purposes of the session is to learn how to manage your discomfort by refocusing on touch sensations. Rather than talking or laughing when you are feeling anxious, try returning the focus of your attention to temperature, pressure, and texture. As you practice this, you may not feel as nervous and you may be less likely to talk or giggle. Additional strategies might include the suggestion of taking a deep breath.

Although talking and sharing is often included in Sensate Focus 2 suggestions, it is discouraged while clients are mastering the basic concepts and skills associated with Sensate Focus 1. The goal of the initial Sensate Focus suggestions is to keep things as simple as possible so clients will succeed. The more types of sensory information they process, in this case, auditory if it involves talking, the more complex the sessions become. Therefore, one of the preliminary suggestions is to keep other sensory input to a minimum. Second, talking and sharing often stimulates more analytical and conscious portions of the brain, and the whole purpose of the initial Sensate Focus exercises is to move away from conscious analysis into sensory experience. Showing and telling, other than within the parameters set by the clinician, are discouraged.

There are two exceptions to talking during Sensate Focus 1 sessions. The first is when one person has finished touching and signals the desire to "Switch" during the session or "Stop" at the end of the session. The second is when anxiety peaks in the touching and then the use of a code word and a change of action are encouraged to manage the anxiety and move through it. The code word should be chosen by the couple prior to the session, and should be positive or neutral in nature. Examples include "change" or "something else." The idea is for clients to acknowledge their anxiety, communicate it, but then move beyond it in a productive, refocusing way rather than stopping the session at that point.

Clothing Options

Initial Sensate Focus includes the suggestion that participants wear little if any clothing during the touching sessions. This is to reduce the likelihood that clients will interpret the removal of clothes as a seductive prelude to a sensual or sexual encounter, thereby placing demands on themselves to feel romantic or sexually stimulated. It is also useful in the desensitization of modesty and an opening to physical and emotional vulnerability. However, as with all suggestions, this one can be changed to include nightwear or underwear, or any other covering on any part of the body, necessary to allay anxiety as much as possible. This is especially true in the early Sensate Focus sessions or when initiating the next level of touching sessions in which additional parts of the body are added to the touch or new positions are assumed. This is most relevant when working with trauma survivors.

Abiding by the Limitations

As Sensate Focus progresses, partners may alternate who is doing the touching (by saying "Switch") and who is stopping the touching (by saying "Stop"), or they may modify it according to their needs and the instructions offered. However, they are encouraged to do *no more* than is suggested by the therapist. This includes engaging in anything that means something sexual to them, or adding on more touching sessions than is suggested by the clinician. More touching sessions are not necessarily more therapeutic.

Throughout the sessions, kissing and full-body contact are discouraged in order to reduce expectations that the touching is supposed to be romantic or sexual. Another limitation is that the person touching is guided to use only fingers, palms, and backs of hands. If arousal occurs, clients are encouraged to take note of this very natural experience but asked to take no further action.

Upon hearing the limitations put on the touching sessions, most people's anxiety immediately goes down. They say things like, "I was able to really touch without worrying because I knew nothing else could happen. It was such a relief." Not only does this ban help remove pressure but it also uses the paradoxical nature of sex as a natural function to the couple's advantage: just as responsiveness is less likely to occur if there is a demand for it, it is also more likely to occur if it is restricted.

Specific Suggestions

Initially, Sensate Focus 1 begins with a clear verbal invitation by the partner who touches first. (These specific suggestions are outlined in Appendix B). As noted, often the partner with the apparent presenting problem is encouraged to initiate *and* touch first in an effort to nullify pressure from the partner and limit partner rejection. However, this can be changed with client input. For example, sometimes a client might be comfortable initiating but would prefer to have the partner touch them first.

Regardless of who initiates, the couple begins the session in a place where, and any position in which, each partner is comfortable (often lying on the bed in the bedroom). They can adjust that position any time. They may begin lying side by side, one person may be kneeling above or next to the partner, or one person may be standing next to the bed while the partner is lying down. Both the person touching (*Toucher*) and the person being touched (*Touchee*) can modify their positions as they desire. The Toucher touches long enough to allow his or her mind to move from everyday thoughts to the more sensory-oriented focus, but not so long that he or she gets bored or tired. A suggested time frame is about 5 to 15 minutes for each partner to touch but, again, clients are strongly urged to avoid looking at the clock. Partners are encouraged to lie next to each other when the session ends.

Clients are initially encouraged to refrain from discussing the sessions as they are lying together or immediately afterwards. This is because the tendency is to move to evaluating the session rather than just staying with the sensory experience.

Writing Down Touching Session Information

Rather than talking about the touching session, clients are encouraged, as soon as possible after each session, to write down specific information about the touching opportunities. Making these notes reinforces focusing on the reliable information that will be most helpful for resolving their sexual concerns, namely, the touch sensations and managing distractions. The specific information includes three types of experiences.

Focusing on Sensations

On what were you able to focus during the sessions? On what sensations were you able to focus, and where? Were you able to touch for your own sensory interest meaning were you able to focus on temperature, pressure, and texture? For example, what was the temperature of your partner's left hand as opposed to his or her right upper arm? These questions are aimed at assessing whether clients are able to touch for their own interest because if they are able to describe sensations then they are touching for themselves as opposed to for their partners.

Distractions
What were some of the distractions (defined as anything other than temperature, pressure, and texture) towards which your attention moved? Some examples might be, "Am I doing this right?", "Is my partner having a good time?", "I forgot to buy milk at the grocery store!" These questions are intended to assess the types of distractions experienced by clients, especially the extent to which they are evaluating their experiences.

Managing Distractions
When you noticed your mind wandering to anything other than the touch sensations, what did you do? Were you able to focus back on the sensations and, if so, on what sensations, and where? These questions are designed to assess whether clients are actively managing distractions.

The importance of thinking about and writing down this information as soon as possible after the sessions cannot be overemphasized. This encourages clients to be descriptive with the information they bring to therapy (the sensations) rather than judgmental (how good or bad it was). It also provides the therapist with precise information about what the Sensate Focus opportunity was like for the clients. By the time participants arrive at the therapy session, they have a tendency not only to forget the details of their experiences during the touching sessions but also to speak in general, conceptual, or evaluative terms when describing the experiences in the therapy session. They are likely to report things like, "The session was fine," "Everything went well," "She felt the same all over," and "We did what you said." This information is not helpful and tells the therapist very little about how the participants actually experienced the Sensate Focus opportunities. The more concrete the information they have written down following the touching sessions, the more likely the therapist will have a subjective frame of reference for what Sensate Focus was like experientially for the clients, and the more likely the therapist will know precisely the next steps to suggest. This benefits the participants by moving Sensate Focus along as productively and as efficiently as possible.

Self-Focus vs. Partner Focus
During the Sensate Focus sessions, the Toucher has contact with the partner while focusing on his or her own sensory experience in a mindful way. The Touchee is also focused on his or her experience of the touching. This point is emphasized frequently.

Handriding, and Positive Handriding
Touching for your interest is different from selfishness because the partner's experience is not ignored. In fact, one of the Touchee's responsibilities while being touched is to non-verbally move the Toucher's hand away from any area the person being touched experiences as physically uncomfortable, extremely emotionally uncomfortable, or ticklish. Alternately, the Touchee can temporarily place his or her hand over or under the Toucher's hand to

regain a greater sense of control as needed. This is referred to as *handriding.* This does not mean that the Toucher cannot return to that area at some later point in the touching. This is a good example of practicing the mindful attitude: the person being touched may experience the same touch in the same area quite differently at another time, and the person touching is practicing the mindful attitude to touching the partner.

Later, *positive handriding* is added. This assists the person being touched to communicate about what he or she *might find interesting* for the Toucher to touch. The Touchee places one hand on top of or underneath the Toucher's hand, indicates the way in which he or she might be interested in having the Toucher touch in terms of location, degree of pressure, and type of motion, and then removes his or her hand after a few seconds.

The Purpose of Handriding and Positive Handriding

Handriding not only protects the person being touched but also, when positive handriding is added, allows him or her to indicate non-demand, exploratory preferences. All of this also frees the person touching to focus on his or her own experience without having to be concerned about distressing the Touchee. This is because the person touching knows as a result of handriding that the person being touched will let him or her know if anything is uncomfortable or, eventually, of interest.

In the absence of any feedback from the Touchee, the Toucher can explore the partner's body for his or her own interest. If the person being touched moves the Toucher's hand, the Toucher is encouraged to interpret this not as a failure to touch *correctly* but rather as a compliment from the Touchee who feels trusting enough to share critical information about self-protection and self-interest. This allows the Toucher to cultivate a more healthy self-focused attitude, free to explore the partner's body without having to worry about whether the Touchee is comfortable or not. It is also easier for the Touchee to become absorbed in the sensations of being touched because he or she is reassured that the Toucher will respond to the handriding directions. It is difficult to say "Yes" to becoming absorbed in the touch for your own interest if you cannot say "No" to it.

Both handriding and positive handriding are intended to foster a positive feedback loop of trust with touching. This non-verbal communication is especially critical in cases of low desire and sexual trauma where partners being touched must perceive themselves as having more control over the touching than may be the case with other clients.

Touching for Interest vs. Pleasure

While touching the partner, the Toucher focuses on his or her own sensory experience by turning attention to the reliable sensations of temperature (cool or warm), pressure (hard or soft), and texture (smooth or rough). This means that the person touching is doing so with a non-demand attitude of interest, curiosity, and exploration rather than with a goal-oriented, pleasuring mindset. This is the *complete opposite of a massage* during which the person touching contacts the partner's body with the expressed intent of trying to make relaxation, enjoyment, or pleasure happen for the Touchee.

However, it is not just the Toucher who is focusing on sensations for his or her own interest. Besides moving the Toucher's hand away if something is physically uncomfortable, the other responsibility of the person being touched is to focus on the tactile sensations wherever the person touching is having contact with his or her body. This includes the Touchee's taking notice of the temperature, pressure, and texture wherever the Toucher's hand is placed.

The Toucher is encouraged to touch long enough to get over any initial discomfort, but not so long as to get tired or bored. Either partner can say, "Switch," and the Toucher becomes the Touchee. When the second partner has finished touching, then he or she may say, "Stop," and the partners complete the session by lying next to one another. While it is usually the second Toucher who ends the sessions, it is also helpful to suggest that either partner can always say, "Stop" at any point during the Sensate Focus exercise. While the couple is encouraged to do no more than is suggested, they are also told that they can always do less. This is, once again, intended to remove pressure to produce any particular emotion, including arousal.

Managing Distractions Through Cognitive-Behavioral Mindfulness

Each person is encouraged to manage distractions by practicing a mindful redirection of attention away from the distractions and back onto an awareness of the dependable and available touch sensations. This combination of what could be described as cognitive-behavioral mindfulness involves bringing attention back to the touch sensations whenever there is a distraction but especially whenever attention wanders to anxiety-provoking thoughts. The person being touched also has the option of managing pressuring distractions by moving the Toucher's hand away if anything is uncomfortable or ticklish. This helps the Toucher manage distractions having to do with concerns about causing the Touchee discomfort or ticklishness.

Clients are informed that it is, in fact, impossible to continuously focus on any one thing, including sensations. The way the brain works is that attention is always jumping from one thing to another. The important skill in Sensate Focus is not to prevent thinking about other things but to recognize and practice refocusing attention when it drifts onto other things besides sensations.

Hierarchy of Exercises

Sensate Focus was originally designed as a hierarchy of relatively invariant touching exercises, using the power of physiological tension that builds by both increasing sensory touch and also limiting sexual release to the couples' advantage. In this manual, instructions for implementing Sensate Focus 1 will follow this hierarchy. *We recommend not only that clients complete each level of the hierarchy before proceeding onto the next one but also that they include all of the previous levels in each of the subsequent touching sessions.* This allows time for couples to cultivate a non-demand, non-pressuring mindset at the beginning of each touching session.

Having said that, the hierarchy of touching suggestions is nonetheless not invariant. It is subject to adjustment based on the goals, values, and sexual practices of the couples. The decisions about changes in the hierarchy are made in discussion between the therapists and clients. The specific sexual difficulty reported by the couple, and the unique individual and couple dynamics, will dictate the structure, pacing, and processing of changes in the order of the touching sessions. Individual and couple dynamics are addressed *in vivo* as partner pressure, avoidance, couple conflicts, or pressuring for goal-oriented achievements arise. This is the art of using Sensate Focus in sex therapy.

Usually clients in Sensate Focus 1 complete the hierarchy before initiating Sensate Focus 2. In this sense, Sensate Focus 1 is like systematic desensitization as the clients are introduced in a small, step-wise fashion to increasingly anxiety-provoking experiences. They are then given the provided therapeutic skills for managing and, therefore, desensitizing themselves to these anxieties while increasing their level of comfort. As a result of the incremental nature of the exercises, coupled with the skills, clients are less likely to fail. Success is simply practice, regardless of the immediate results. If they interpret themselves as unsuccessful, their experience is reframed as a learning opportunity, and the roadblocks are processed.

Individual Self-Discovery and Touch

Although working with couples is emphasized, an individual may present alone for sex therapy, or the presenting sexual concern may prompt individual touching sessions for one or both members of the couple (see Illustrations 5.1, 5.2, and 5.3.).

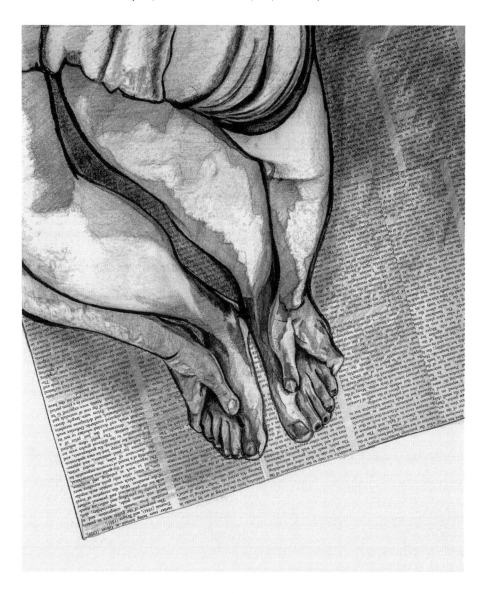

5.1

Individual Self-Discovery
and Touch

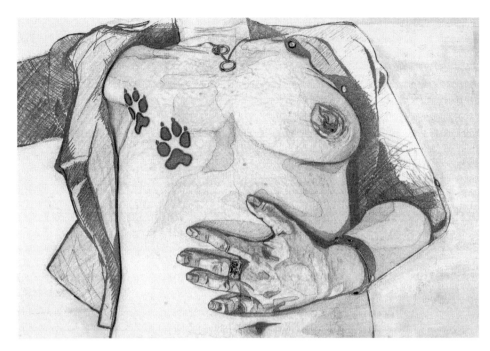

5.2
Individual Self-Discovery
and Touch

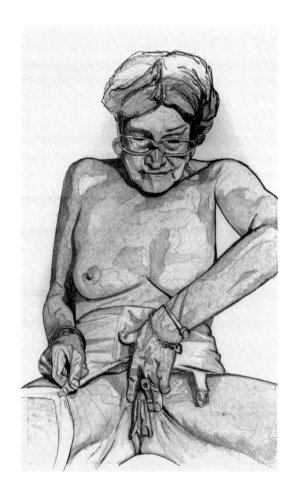

5.3
Individual Self-Discovery and Touch

For example, cases of Penetration Disorder (Vaginismus), Premature/Delayed Ejaculation, or sexual trauma often benefit from focusing on the individual at least at the beginning of treatment. The identified client, who may be extremely anxious, is provided an opportunity to develop an increased level of comfort and skill with touching for self-interest prior to being introduced to the greater complexities associated with the couple's Sensate Focus. Self-Sensate Focus is the same as systematic desensitization in that the client is introduced in a step-wise fashion to potentially increasing anxiety-provoking situations.

The individual begins self-Sensate Focus in much the same way as when touching the partner during the couple opportunities, touching all over the body while avoiding breast, chest, and genital contact or contact with any area of the body that represents something sexually or emotionally uncomfortable (see Illustrations 5.2 and 5.3.). The skills are exactly the same as when the couple is involved. The individual client focuses on the touch sensations of temperature, pressure, and texture, only in this case when touching his or her own body. The client is both the Toucher *and* the Touchee. This is handled by having clients focus on the sensations in their hands wherever they are touching themselves.

When clients involved in self-Sensate Focus report decreased apprehensions, are able to report details of tactile sensations from touching different areas of his/her body, and are adept at managing distractions by refocusing on these touch sensations, they can be encouraged to incorporate breasts, chest, and genitals into the contact. If or when touching becomes too anxiety provoking, these clients can move away from touching breasts, chest, and/or genitals. Suggestions may include having as many as one self-touching session a day, schedule permitting, but usually no more than six in a seven-day period.

When clients are engaged in self-Sensate Focus, they allow the focus of their attention to move to the touch sensations in their body wherever they are touching. If their attention seems to move primarily on either their hands with which they are touching, or on where they are touching, they are encouraged to intentionally move their attention to the other source of sensations.

Breasts/Chest and Genitals Off Limits

When describing the following positions to couples, it is helpful to let them know, "There is nothing magical about the positions. The positions are not going to make anything happen in and of themselves. Instead, they merely provide reasonably comfortable ways partners can touch as much of each other as possible without Touchers having to move too much."

The couple's phase of Sensate Focus 1 begins with *breasts, chest, and genitals off limits* (see illustrations 5.4, 5.5, and 5.6.). *We highly recommend having all couple's sessions begin with this touching component* in order to allow time for cultivating a non-demand, touching for one's interest, mindset. The person touching has contact with all of the partner's body, front and back, avoiding breasts, chest, and genitals (and any other part of the partner's body that, to the couple, represents something sexual). The person touching focuses on his or her own experience of the different temperatures, textures, and pressures of the partner's skin and hair, and brings attention mindfully back to these sensations when distracted.

5.4
Breasts/Chest and Genitals Off Limits, Lying on Back

When clients are able to touch for self-interest, focusing on sensations, and bringing themselves back from anxiety-provoking distractions, they begin Sensate Focus with breasts, chest,
and genitals included. If they are not ready, they may stay at the breasts and genitals off limits
stage with the addition of water soluable, non-lanolin, hypoallergenic lotions to vary the sensations and to signify that progress is being made. However, the lotion is not intended to suggest
a demand attitude to produce arousal or any other kind of pleasure; instead, it is a tool for
increasing variations in the touch sensations.

Handriding

It is during the initial touching sessions when breasts/chest and genitals are off limits that
handriding is introduced. As suggested, if and when the clients who are being touched

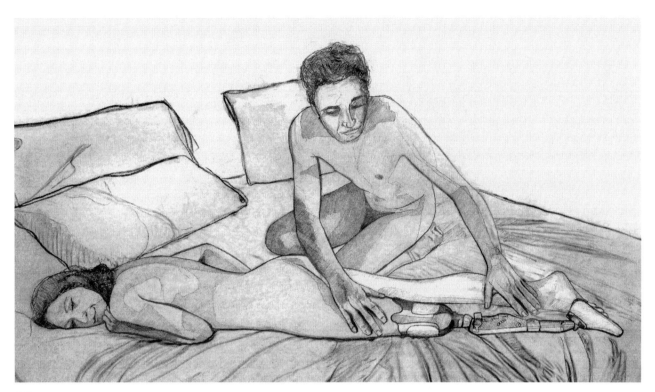

5.5

Breasts/Chest and Genitals Off Limits, Lying on Front

experience anything as physically uncomfortable, highly emotionally uncomfortable, or ticklish, they are to move the Toucher's hand away from that area, or place his or her hand under or over the Toucher's hand for a moment to regain a sense of control. The person being touched places his or her hand on the hand of the person touching for a few seconds, moves it away from the uncomfortable area for that moment, and then takes the hand off the Toucher's hand since the person touching is still primarily directing the touching. As suggested, this not only protects the Touchee from having to grin and bear any distressing touch but also frees up the Toucher to touch for his or her own interest without having to be concerned about the partner's experience.

Breasts/Chest and Genitals On Limits

When both partners are able to touch for their own interest and bring themselves back from distraction with breasts, chest, and genitals off limits, the breasts, chest, and genitals are added into the touch (see Illustrations 5.7, 5.8, and 5.9.). The couple begins the Sensate Focus opportunities as before, touching initially with breasts, chest, and genitals off limits until they are centered on tactile sensations. Then breasts, chest, and external genital touching are incorporated into the touch, and full-body touching for self-interest begins. Clients are encouraged to attend to changes in sensory experience, not to stay focused solely on the breasts, chest, or genitals once these are on limits, and to move away from and then back to these areas in order to have a full-body touching experience. This moving around to all

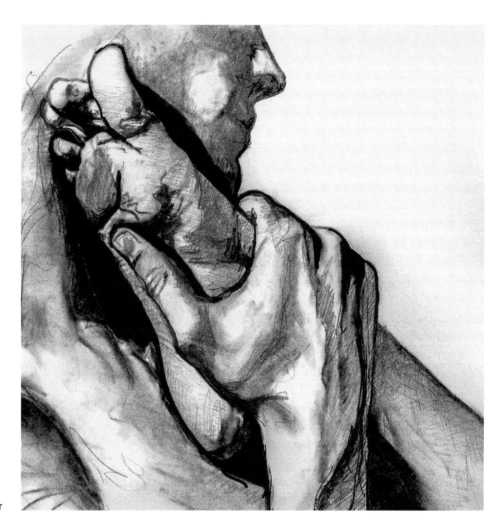

5.6
Breasts/Chest and Genitals
Off Limits, Touching All Over

areas of the body also serves the purpose of moderating anxiety associated with touching any particular part of the body.

Positions

The couple is offered two positions when breasts, chest, and genital touching are added (see Illustrations 5.7 and 5.8.). In the first position, the Toucher sits up with the back against a headboard or wall, supportive pillows behind, and legs spread out in front in a "V" shape. The person being touched lies on his or her back between the Toucher's outspread legs, face towards the ceiling, genitals close but not touching the other person's genitals, with knees bent, calves up and over the partner's thighs, and feet placed down on the outside of the partner's hips.

If the person being touched feels too exposed or vulnerable in this first position, the Touchee can sit between the Toucher's outspread legs, with the back up against the Toucher's chest, both partners facing forward, and with the Touchee's legs draped over the Toucher's in a wider "V" (see Illustration 5.9). We sometimes described this as the

5.7

Breasts/Chest and Genitals On Limits, One Partner Sitting Up, the Other Lying Down

motorcycle position with the person being touched in the front. The person touching can reach around the partner's body to include the breasts, chest, and external genitals into the contact.

Managing Arousal

Initially, if either partner experiences arousal, he or she is encouraged to do one or a combination of things. First, since one of the purposes of Sensate Focus is to allow clients to experience and be aware of their arousal in a non-demand way, if either or both become excited,

5.8

Breasts/Chest and Genitals On Limits, One Partner Sitting Up, the Other Lying Down

they are invited to attend to their arousal as it is, until and unless it becomes uncomfortable or distracting.

If or when arousal becomes uncomfortable, extremely distracting, or is experienced as goal-oriented, the Touchee may choose to handride the Toucher's hands away from that area so that this does not become a focused, demand distraction. If visual sensations become overly stimulating, clients are encouraged to close their eyes.

If the Toucher is touching for self-focused interest, and if the Touchee is absorbed in the sensations, the Touchee may, in fact, become orgasmic. This is not a problem because, again, just as sexual responsiveness cannot be made to happen, it can also not be prevented from happening. Therefore, as long as being orgasmic is not the intention of the Touchee or the Toucher, it is framed positively in terms of natural function, and the partners are encouraged to continue on with the Sensate Focus exercise. If a male partner has ejaculated, he can use a towel to dry off but then return his focus to other touch sensations. Being orgasmic is the one time *not* to stop the Sensate Focus session. This is to reinforce the notion that there is no necessary connection between a specific sexual response and anything in particular having to happen as a result of that response.

5.9
Breasts/Chest and Genitals On Limits, Both Partners Sitting Up, One in Front

Moving from Absorbed <u>In</u> Sensations to Absorbed <u>By</u> Sensations (or Sensuality)
It is at this point that the Sensate Focus 1 attitude of touching for one's interest begins to dovetail with the Sensate Focus 2 attitude of touching to include both focusing on the other person as well as moving beyond absorption *in* sensations into absorption *by* sensations. Focusing on and being absorbed *in* sensations is the precursor to losing awareness of and being absorbed *by* sensations. Being absorbed *by* sensations might be described as the *subjective experience of sensuality*. This experience of sensuality in turn *is what ultimately serves as the most powerful portal into sexual responsiveness.* As the sensual experience of absorption by the sensations results in the loss of consciousness as to sensations and

even time and place, the client is highly likely to be carried along into sexual arousal and pleasure.

During this absorption, the Toucher can continue to touch in the area that appears to be arousing or pleasurable for the Touchee as long as the Toucher can do so for his or her own interest, and as long as the person being touched does not move the Toucher's hand away or transition into a goal-oriented mindset.

When the experience of becoming absorbed by the sensations washes over the clients, an "oops" may occur when the couple goes beyond the suggestions, perhaps even to intercourse. This is managed by normalizing their desire to go with their arousal and delight, but then they are encouraged to return to the guidelines in order to keep the Sensate Focus sessions from becoming goal-oriented and losing its effectiveness.

Clinical Look

Generally after the first experience of breasts, chest, and genitals on limits, clients are asked to do a *clinical look* at their own and/or each other's genitals (see Illustration 5.10). If one or both report being unfamiliar with their own genitals, the individual clinical look is conducted first. With some lighting on, clients are asked to look at and explore their genitals first by themselves and then eventually with one another. The main purpose is for them to identify the different areas of their genitals. For example, in the case of women, they identify the

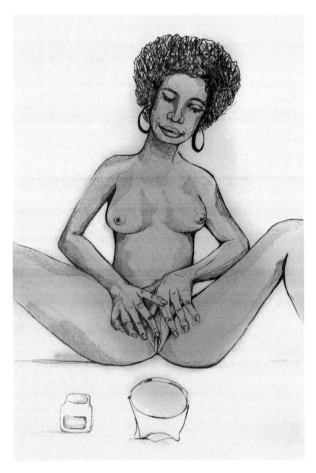

5.10
Clinical Look

location of their clitoris, the clitoral shaft, and the inner and outer labia. This experience not only gives them a chance to gather accurate information about their genitals but it also brings about a sense of intimate sharing and breaking down barriers of ignorance and discomfort. It promotes more disclosure in Sensate Focus 1 of what is of interest to each, and in Sensate Focus 2 of what is pleasing.

Mutual Touching

When partners can touch for their own interest, focus on sensations and bring themselves back from distractions when breasts, chest, and genitals are added, the couple moves on to include mutual touching (see Illustrations 5.11, 5.12, and 5.13). Partners lie next to each other, sit facing each other, or get into any other position with which they are comfortable and that

5.11
Mutual Touching,
Breasts/Chest and
Genitals Off Limits,
Lying Facing Partner

5.12
Mutual Touching, Sitting Facing Each Other, Breasts/Chest and Genitals Off Limits or On Limits

allows them to touch each other as completely as possible. They begin to touch each other at the same time for their own interest. At first they avoid breasts, chest, and genitals until they are able to focus easily on the sensations in this position.

Eventually clients include the breasts, chest, and genitals into the mutual touching as they would any other part of the body, focusing on temperature, pressure, and texture. Mutual touching may not be as easy as it sounds because now they are receiving sensation from two sources simultaneously: where they are touching; and where they are being touched. Clients are confronted with a dynamic tension between different demands for their attention. They are encouraged to let their attention go where it will, but if they are noticing themselves primarily focused on where they are touching, they also move their attention to where they are being touched, and vice versa. They are now learning to focus alternately on each source of stimulation until the sensations meld into a global absorption. In this way, they are learning to honor the space between them and the interaction that connects them.

5.13
Mutual Touching, Breasts/Chest and Genitals On Limits, Lying Facing Partner

We have emphasized touching at the same time during the mutual touching. However, clients are encouraged to alternate between touching simultaneously and touching each other one at a time. Just because mutual touching has been put on limits does not mean that clients always have to be touching simultaneously. This reinforces the fact that the touching is increasingly an organic dance between the partners.

Positive Handriding

Up to this point the person being touched has been encouraged to either move the Toucher's hand away, or to handride the Toucher's hand, if there is anything the Toucher is doing that

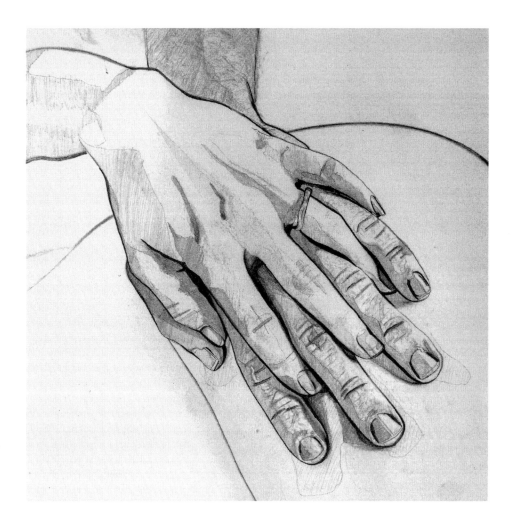

5.14
Positive Handriding

is uncomfortable or ticklish. During mutual touching, if not earlier during breasts, chests, and genitals on limits, a *positive handriding* suggestion is added.

Positive handriding involves the Touchee's placing one hand on top of or underneath the Toucher's hand, lacing fingers in between the Toucher's fingers (see Illustration 5.14 and 5.15). Then the Touchee briefly uses this hand to move the Toucher's hand not only *away from* areas that might be uncomfortable or ticklish but also *towards* areas that might be of interest to the Touchee.

The person being touched keeps the hand on or under the Toucher's hand for a *few seconds*, and then takes it away since the person touching is still, for the most part, in charge of directing the touching. The Touchee may also demonstrate interest in being touched with lighter or firmer pressure or a different kind of motion. In essence, positive handriding is used to suggest location, degree of pressure, and type of motion.

It is critical that the therapist choose words carefully when describing positive handriding at the risk of its being interpreted as a technique for producing pleasure, relaxation, arousal, or orgasm. The person touching is counseled to move the Toucher's hand to some area of the body the Touchee might find *interesting* or *of interest.* These words are recommended

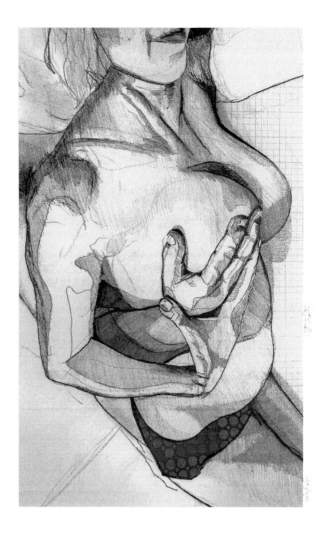

5.15
Positive Handriding on Breasts or Chest

because *interest* has already been defined as exploring temperature, pressure, and texture in the moment. Interest does not involve trying to force specific emotional responses.

Positive handriding allows the person being touched to do several things. First, it gives the Touchee a greater sense of control. Second, it facilitates experimenting with touch sensations in particularly sensitive areas of the body.

Positive handriding also expands the Touchee's non-verbal communicative repertoire from merely conveying what he or she *doesn't* find comfortable to also conveying what he or she *might* find of interest. But it does something that is perhaps even more important: it initiates a more complex and eventually reciprocal form of communication between the partners (in this case, non-verbal) that lays the groundwork for Sensate Focus 2. Now clients can provide accurate information to each other about both what they don't want as well as what they do want. When partners do this at the same time, they begin to move beyond the goal of working on the sexual dysfunction and towards intimacy enhancement.

As suggested, although positive handriding is often introduced during the mutual touching phase of Sensate Focus, it can be added earlier or later depending on the needs of the couple. As with all other aspects of Sensate Focus, there is no one time to use any particular skill, and no one way to apply that skill.

Partner Astride, Genital-to-Genital Contact Without Insertion

The next Sensate Focus experience is mutual touching with the addition of, in the case of heterosexual couples, the woman's going astride her partner (see Illustration 5.16). Once again, it is highly recommended that the sessions do not start with this position but include all the previous positions in the hierarchy to allow for the cultivation of a non-demand, here-and-now mindset.

The astride position involves the client's hovering over and facing the partner, her knees on the bed, supporting herself with her knees close to her partner's body and with her non-dominant hand positioned above one of her partner's shoulders, supporting herself in a tri-pod fashion with both knees and one hand. This leaves her other hand free. She does not sit directly on the partner, nor does she lie down. Rather, she hovers above at a 45-degree angle, much like a jockey on a horse. She is encouraged to use her partner's genitals much as she would use her own hand, exploring vulvar, clitoral, and *mons* contact using her partner's

5.16
Partner Astride Without Insertion

genitals but without insertion. She keeps going with the attitude of touching for focused self-interest and redirecting attention back to sensations.

Placing a pillow under the knees of the astride partner may be helpful for elevation when the astride partner is significantly shorter or the partner on the bottom significantly broader. In the case of same-sex couples, the positions for genital-to-genital contact can be modified according to the couple's preferences, body fit and comfort. Lesbian couples may choose to lie flat on top of the partner, or assume a scissoring position. Male couples may stand or kneel facing each other and utilize genital-to-genital contact in these or any comfortable position.

While the client who is astride is focusing on the touch sensations of genital-to-genital contact, the other partner on the bottom has two responsibilities. The first is to refrain from any hip movement ("Your hips are led!"), and the second is to leave the genital-to-genital contact to the astride partner while focusing on the touch sensations wherever his or her hands are touching different parts of the astride partner's body.

The astride partner may not be able to remain in this position for more than a few minutes before tiring. The couple is encouraged to change position when this occurs. They may resume touching in any of the earlier positions from mutual touching to my turn/your turn touching before resuming the astride, genital-to-genital touching at least one or two additional times.

When genital-to-genital contact in the astride position is paired with the preceding sensory experiences and the prohibition against doing anything intentional with any arousal, there can be a harkening back to earlier, and often exciting taboo-filled, experiences of youthful, playful exploration. It is difficult for most people not to experience arousal if this becomes the case.

However, with couples presenting with arousal or orgasmic difficulties, expectations for response may be amplified when genital-to-genital contact is included. The expectations and/ or the natural waxing and waning of arousal that may occur in this position may rekindle what are referred to as *fears of performance*. Fears of performance are apprehensions about whether or not arousal or orgasm will occur. They are often accompanied by *spectatoring*, the observation of whether or not one is aroused or approaching orgasm. These fears of performance and spectatoring are addressed, providing the opportunity to discuss the fact that the partner with lower anxiety is perfectly capable of being orgasmic even when the anxiety-wrought partner is experiencing little or no arousal. This is particularly important for men suffering from erectile insecurity: It assures them that the partners' absorption, arousal, and even orgasm do not depend on their penile engorgement. Therapists can offer a paradoxical injunction suggesting that clients intentionally allow for the gaining, losing, and regaining of arousal. This may interrupt fears of losing arousal and provides an opportunity for teaching skills to manage anxiety. It also frees both partners to experiment in terms of what they can attend to in ways that they most likely have never experienced before or at least not since they were much younger. All of this may evoke a previously unbeknownst or forgotten sexual vitality.

Partner Astride, Genital-to-Genital Contact With Insertion

Additional suggestions in the astride position may include insertion without movement, absorbing the sensations while resisting a goal-oriented agenda (see Illustration 5.17). The partner lying down is encouraged to keep the pelvis still throughout this stage. With heterosexual partners, the female client gets in the astride position and is encouraged to take her

5.17
Partner Astride With Insertion

partner's penis and do the inserting. This is for three reasons: she knows when she is ready; she knows when her partner is ready; and she knows where it goes. We are fond of saying, "There are no eyes on the head of the penis so the penis does not know precisely where the vaginal opening is located and when the vagina is ready."

The astride partner is encouraged to insert the penis slowly, a little bit at a time. The clients are both urged to attend to the tactile sensations during each stage of insertion rather than on judgments of whether or not it feels good, whether either is aroused or not, or on any other distracting thoughts. Full engorgement is not necessary to incorporate this suggestion. In cases in which arousal or engorgement is lost or diminished as the couple engages in genital-to-genital contact with the possibility of insertion, this may be framed as an excellent learning opportunity that illustrates that fears of performance and spectatoring are to be expected, that they affect sexual responsiveness, and that they can be managed through refocusing on sensations and using the code word.

Insertion Without Movement

Once there is full insertion, the partners focus on the sensations associated with penile containment, allowing the sensations to wash over them but without any movement. This gives partners the chance to experience the sensations of insertion without any demands for arousal or activity. We advise them that without movement, arousal may diminish. In fact, they are encouraged to stay in this position until there is loss of whatever arousal and engorgement is present if arousal and engorgement happen. Many clients report feeling very emotionally connected after this exercise and for many it is quite erotic. For men with erectile insecurity, the experience of being asked to lose their engorgement on purpose is often revolutionary.

Insertion With Movement

If insertion takes place, the astride partner is encouraged to explore different types of movement. Clients may explore movement with insertion as long as this is done while focusing on sensations for self-interest and not with any expectations for arousal or pleasure. Most couples have never taken the opportunity to experience insertion in an interest-focused, non-demand fashion. Once there is insertion, many partners often think arousal and orgasm are the inevitable goal. They miss delving into sensory exploration in this position for its own sake.

While the astride partner is tending to the genital-to-genital sensations, she can also focus on touching other parts of her partner's body, and her partner can continue to focus on the sensations wherever his hands are touching her. Once again, however, the partner on the bottom has the responsibilities of refraining from moving his hips and of leaving the genital-to-genital contact to her. As before, the astride partner is to alternate between being in the astride position, and getting off and into the mutual touching or any earlier my turn/ your turn position.

Lying Next to Each Other Afterwards, and Options for Release

When the touching session ends, either partner can say "Stop." Partners are encouraged to lie next to each other following the session (see Illustration 5.18). The couple may talk, practice mindfulness, or experience the power of being non-verbally present with the other person but without the pressure of achieving any particular goal.

Sensate Focus participants are encouraged throughout the initial Sensate Focus exercises to avoid intentionally trying to be orgasmic either during or apart from the touching sessions. This is intended to allow sexual tension to percolate over the course of treatment, taking advantage of the fact that the more sexual responsiveness is restricted, the more likely it is to occur. Clients are usually willing to accept this ban on orgasm if treatment is intensive.

However, if therapy is in a weekly outpatient setting, or takes a longer time, clients may be less likely to follow the ban. If this is the case, there are options for release. For example, if

5.18
Lying With Each Other After Touching

one member of the couple feels aroused even after lying quietly with the partner for a while, this client may indicate he or she would like orgasmic release. But in an effort to encourage collaboration and communication, it is suggested that the other choose one of three alternatives for providing release. The partner may: (1) inform the person asking for release that the partner prefers for that person to provide his or her own release in private; (2) lie next to and hold or touch the person asking for release while that person provides his or her own release with manual stimulation; or (3) provide manual release for the person seeking release. Oral release is discouraged because this tends to trigger expectations for a more goal-oriented, sexual or pleasuring encounter. It also may trigger prior pressure dynamics between the partners.

Couples may be reminded that they can actually do whatever they would like following the touching sessions. However, the purpose of sex therapy and Sensate Focus at this point is to build sexual tension and reduce goal-oriented pressure. Couples may not see progress with the dysfunction until and unless this tension is allowed to strengthen and they have had an opportunity to integrate the Sensate Focus skills and attitudes.

5.19

Lying With Each Other After

Touching

Another option for release is to propose that the couple engages in any desired sexual activity but that this is entirely separate from the Sensate Focus sessions. Otherwise, a pattern may emerge in which Sensate Focus is experienced as pressured. Sexual activity apart from Sensate Focus opportunities is often most helpful when therapy takes place once a week or less frequently, extending it over a longer period of time. An average of 14 therapy appointments is often necessary to proceed through all of the Sensate Focus 1 sessions. However, these may be scheduled less often as the couple progresses.

The Paradox of Powerful Presence

The profundity of shifting from an attitude of trying to control sexual and pleasurable responses for oneself and especially for one's partner, to one of honoring sexual and pleasurable responses as natural functions by redirecting attention away from anxiety-producing expectations, onto present sensations in a mindful way, and for one's own interest, cannot be overstated. It moves clients away from using Sensate Focus as a demand-oriented technique aimed at generating self and partner pleasure, an attitude that only adds to their pressures and problems. It moves clients towards reducing pressure and expectations by focusing on that over which they have control (the ability to direct attention to sensations). By focusing on these sensations, clients are guided to a powerful gateway into the very experiences for which they ultimately have sought therapy, namely, arousal, pleasure, and fostering greater intimacy.

Chapter 6: Processing Sensate Focus 1 Instructions

When the couple returns to the therapist's office for the next scheduled session, each partner's experience is processed according to some helpful guidelines. This ensures that the therapist has a concrete sense of the clients' subjective experiences and an ongoing window into their individual and relationship dynamics. While therapy sessions emphasize the specifics of Sensate Focus, they may also include an overview of the clients' general life experiences, stresses, and relationship and communication skills, challenges, and successes since the last therapy session. As it is the intent of this manual to discuss the specifics of the touching sessions, we will leave it to others and to later publications to elucidate the details of any individual and/or relationship therapy that may accompany sex therapy.

In terms of processing the Sensate Focus suggestions, it usually works best to have one partner describe his or her experience first while the other is encouraged to listen, if only for the practical reason that it is difficult for the therapist to attend to two people's experience at once. It is helpful to alternate who begins talking first in subsequent sessions. This structure affords clients an opportunity to really attend to what the partner experienced during the session, something that many partners have had little chance to do. It is remarkable how differently the Sensate Focus sessions may be experienced by the partners. Often they are confused by these differences, often they are intrigued, and often the therapist learns much about the couple's dynamics, observing how they relate and communicate about these differences in the session. All this helps the therapist steer Sensate Focus, specifically, and sex therapy, generally, in the most productive direction.

Throughout the processing of Sensate Focus opportunities, the therapist listens for whether clients have been able to touch or be touched for themselves rather than for their partner, and whether the clients have been able to touch or be touched for their own interest (focusing on sensations) rather than in service to expectations for arousal or pleasure. The distractions experienced and their handling of them inside and outside the bedroom are also included in the processing.

Touching for Self by Describing One's Experience vs. Focusing on the Partner

The attitude of touching for self is usually evident in two ways. These include the words that are used to describe the touching, and the nature of the distractions.

Words and Their Influence on Attitudes

As we have noted, words can have a powerful influence on the emotions and attitudes clients are experiencing, and whether these emotions and attitudes are more or less productive for resolving the clients' sexual dysfunction. When it comes to processing Sensate Focus suggestions, and when participants use evaluative or partner-oriented expressions like, "It didn't go well because I didn't get an erection," "She seemed to be having a good time," or "He massaged me like he knows I like it," you can be reasonably assured that they are focused on the partner's response during the touching rather than on their own experience in the moment. Attending to the wording is critical in order to catch when clients are expressing this goal- and partner-oriented focus.

Clients may voice frustration in the beginning as the therapist respectfully suggests using different words when describing the Sensate Focus opportunities: "Rather than telling me how you touched him where he likes to be touched, can you *describe* the sensations you experienced when and where you were touching him?" With more practice most clients will soon appreciate the significance of the words and how these words influence their touching attitudes during the actual Sensate Focus sessions.

Distractions

The second way partner focus shows up is by the words the clients choose to describe the distractions they had during the touching sessions. It is important for the therapist to listen for how frequently the clients' minds wander to the other person as they describe what captured their attention other than the sensations. This is true for both the Touchee as well as the Toucher.

Touching for Interest by Describing Sensations vs. Touching for Pleasure by Describing Judgments and Emotions

With regard to assessing participants' ability to focus for *interest* rather than on pleasure or arousal, the therapist may listen for how precisely and vividly the clients describe sensations, and they can also listen for the use of judgmental and emotion-oriented words.

Precise, Vivid Descriptions

A useful question with which to begin is, "Who initiated the session and tell me where you began touching first?" This can be followed up with, "Tell me what sensations you were able to focus in on while you were touching there." The importance of the precision with which clients describe their attention to sensory information cannot be overemphasized. There is a lovely paragraph in Alain de Botton's *How Proust Can Change Your Life* in which the renowned author Marcel Proust has asked a new acquaintance to describe how certain committees work. The acquaintance begins with, "Well we generally meet at 10:00, there are secretaries behind …" and Proust stops him.

> "Mais non, mais non, vous allez trop vite … Vous montez l'escalier. Vous entrez dans la salle … Précisez, mon cher, précisez. [But no, but no, you go too quickly … You climb the stairs. You enter the room … Be precise, my dear, be precise]." So I tell him everything … the rustle of the papers; the tea in the next room; the macaroons.
>
> (de Botton, 1998, p. 46)

As therapists we must be Proustian in our measured attention to the details of sensation descriptions so that our clients will want to divulge everything down to minute details. This is in service not only to the therapist's knowing exactly what suggestions to make but also to the clients' learning a new way of thinking about mindful touching. Although as children we could focus in this here-and-now fashion, most of us as adults have neurologically moved, and have been socialized to move, away from being present in the moment as our brains developed to think more abstractly. While conceptual thinking is beneficial in just about everything else we do as adults, it works against us when it comes to attending to present sensations in such a way as to allow the natural function of sexual responsiveness to express itself. The more intellectually sophisticated the clients, the more difficult this might be for them. Sensate Focus is not actually about teaching people something new so much as it is about helping them re-access aspects of themselves with which they were once in touch and that serve as portals into the natural function of sexual responses.

Given these issues, it is of paramount importance that the therapist vigilantly yet gently keeps redirecting the clients back to descriptions of sensations. "Mais non, mais non, vous allez trop vite. Tell me when you were touching her arm, where on her arm were you touching? Where did you start touching first? And what sensations did you notice? Was that part of her arm cool or warm? Rough or smooth? Where did you touch next? What was the temperature there? Were you aware of pressure? Hardness? Softness? And tell me about the textures in that area." Soon, the participants will become more adept at this mindfulness language and will have less difficulty providing the therapist (as well as themselves) with the sensory information needed to know how to move forward.

Judgmental and Emotion-Oriented Words

The second indicator of the degree to which participants are able to focus for their own interest is the extent to which they use evaluative and emotional language. Listen for words like "good" or "bad," "fine" or "not so great," "pleasurable" or "frustrating," "arousing" or "boring," "relaxing" or "anxiety-provoking," "sensual" or "irritating." These usually suggest clients are touching in order to produce some kind of arousing, pleasurable, relaxing, or enjoyable emotion, or to generate some kind of good or correct experience, and are expecting to be able to produce emotions and feelings of this nature. Depending on having a specific emotion or feeling sets up more pressure and that is exactly the opposite of what Sensate Focus is all about.

While the therapist is not trying to make things uncomfortable for the clients, the therapist is not particularly interested at this point in whether the Sensate Focus session was enjoyable or not, or whether it was good or not. Instead, what the therapist *is* interested in is the clients' descriptions of sensation-oriented words like "cool, warm," "hard, soft," and "rough, smooth" to convey their experiences, and the therapist is also interested in the nature of the distractions and how they were handled.

Identifying Distractions

The next line of discovery in processing the Sensate Focus sessions has to do with distractions. A useful questions is, "What else were you thinking about while you were doing the Sensate Focus exercise?" Not infrequently clients will say, "I wasn't thinking about anything."

Processing Sensate Focus 1 Instructions

This, of course, is impossible. It is easy for clients to consider themselves as having failed at the exercises when they think about anything other than tactile sensations. They must be reassured that not only is it natural to have distractions but also that the distractions provide an opportunity for practicing refocusing on sensations. It may be helpful to remind them that it is human nature to pay attention to a large number of things in rapid succession, so quickly that it seems as if they are concentrating on more than one thing at the same time. For example, one study suggests that the human eyeball processes a couple of hundred bits of information within the first few seconds of entering a new room. And that is just the eyeball! Not only can distractions not be eliminated, they cannot be avoided.

Clients may also respond to questions about distractions with a judgment that their distractions are *wrong*. "I know I shouldn't have been thinking about this, but I started wondering if I shouldn't be getting aroused." Clients often interpret the information that it is not the purpose of Sensate Focus to get arousal or feel pleasured as meaning that if they think about pleasure or find themselves getting aroused they are somehow not following the instructions. They may need to be reassured that, in general, they cannot prevent or eliminate distractions, and also that they cannot experience a "wrong" distraction. Just as teachers of meditation, yoga, and other mindfulness practices remind us, distractions are not bad or wrong; they simply are. If eliminating distractions is impossible, trying to prevent them is also a waste of time. More specifically, when it comes to Sensate Focus, the purpose is not to eliminate distractions such as performance-oriented thoughts, but to work with them regardless of their content, taking note of them as apertures into whether the person is touching for his or her own interest, and then redirecting attention onto sensations.

Managing Distractions

The next line of processing is asking clients what they did during the sessions when they noticed themselves becoming (unavoidably) distracted. It is important not to accept broad or vague statements like, "I did what you suggested," "I managed them well," or "I focused on how I was feeling." The first is general; the second is judgmental; and the third is emotion-oriented. While reminding them that distractions are to be accepted, clients are encouraged to return the focus of their attention to touch sensations. This is just about always the answer to their questions having to do with, "What do I do if … "

One set of instructions that is sometimes confusing involves interpreting and managing positive emotions as distractions. Clients sometimes have difficulty understanding why they are being guided away from focusing on enjoyment, relaxation, and arousal and back onto sensations. A useful way of handling this is to remind them that there is nothing problematic with these distractions *per se*; the issue is that they cannot focus simultaneously, at that precise second in time, on both the positive emotions and the tactile sensations. The presence of positive emotions is not dependable while the presence of sensations is, and these sensations serve as the reliable gateway into the natural function of the positive emotions. They are not discouraged from savoring their relaxation, pleasure, or arousal. However, since these emotions often lead to expectations that they should feel more of them as the touching progresses, they are encouraged to refocus on the sensations as the trustworthy segue into more sustained positive experiences that eventually transform focus on sensations into experiences of being in sensations without conscious awareness.

Moving the Toucher's Hand (Handriding and Positive Handriding)

Some of the most important questions to ask couples when processing Sensate Focus are whether or not the Touchee non-verbally moved the partner's hand away or used handriding at any time during the session and, as Sensate Focus progresses, whether the Touchee used positive handriding. Participants will often have either forgotten these directions or will have interpreted them as suggestions to be used *only if* they are feeling physically uncomfortable or ticklish during the touching opportunity. While this is the ultimate use for handriding and positive handriding, it is helpful in the early stages of Sensate Focus to have the Touchees practice moving the Toucher's hand away and using positive handriding *whether the Touchees need these or not* so that it becomes second nature for Touchees to do this. If people being touched do not practice moving the Toucher's hand even when unnecessary during initial sessions, they are unlikely to remember to use it when they really need or want it.

Chapter 7: Modifications of Sensate Focus 1 for Diverse Client Populations

Sex therapists from a wide variety of mental health and medical professions have creatively expanded the use of Sensate Focus over the years since Masters and Johnson published their work with primarily able-bodied, Caucasian, heterosexual couples. In fact, one of the most fertile areas in the expansion of Masters and Johnson's work has been the use of Sensate Focus with diverse populations (Linschoten, Weiner, & Avery-Clark, 2016). Studies indicate that these additions to Sensate Focus are helpful for meeting the varied needs of people. In this next chapter, we will describe how to tailor Sensate Focus to the specific needs of a greater diversity of populations.

In Clinical Settings

From Intensive to Weekly Sessions

Masters and Johnson practiced short-term intensive therapy that involved seeing couples away from their hometown and meeting daily or several times a day for a 14-day period. They believed this intensive format fostered rapid progress for two reasons. First, social isolation for couples helps them focus on their intimate relationship and limits other obligations and distractions. Second, there is opportunity for numerous and concentrated Sensate Focus sessions. One of the ways to overcome fears of performance through Sensate Focus is to develop such a build-up of physiologic tension resulting from frequent Sensate Focus exercises that it is difficult for sexual desire and arousal to be waylaid by distractions. "With the subject [and experience] of sex exposed to daily consideration, sexual stimulation usually elevates rapidly and accrues to the total relationship" (Masters & Johnson, 1970, p. 17). If the accrual of sexual tension can be coaxed and experienced in the contained setting of an intensive therapeutic arrangement, sexual partners can progress quickly; they have Mother Nature on their side.

For many couples for whom immediate results are critical, this intensive approach continues to be ideal. For those who live in remote locations, travel frequently for work, or find it impossible to shake off responsibilities while at home, sex therapy coupled with social isolation can fan a hot cauldron of change.

However, there are realistic limitations with an intensive format. These include both the clients' obligations outside of the relationship and the therapists' other professional responsibilities. Currently, "The usual practice is for clients to be seen on a once-a-week, 50-minute basis" (McCarthy, 1973, p. 290). Each session includes a review and discussion of the previous week's assignments, processing the clients' feelings, and offering the next set of suggestions.

The advantage of this "elongated therapy period" is that it allows clients "to pace themselves in terms of acceptance of their sexual responses" (McCarthy, 1973, p. 293). It also finesses one difficulty of the intensive format, namely, that couples may have problems with re-entry into their everyday lives. With the once-a-week format, partners can learn to balance job, family, self-care, responsibilities, and other interests while maintaining or resuming their treatment progress at the same time. However, if a rapid, sequestered program is feasible, re-entry problems can be effectively managed with follow-up appointments on a regular or intermittent basis. These check-ups remind partners to set aside quality time, schedule touching on a regular basis, and practice the individual and relationship skills they have learned.

From Dual-Sex Team to Individual Practitioner

The original Masters and Johnson model for Sensate Focus included a dual-sex therapist team with heterosexual couples because

> Controlled laboratory experimentation in human sexual physiology has supported unequivocally the initial investigative premise that no man will ever fully understand woman's sexual function or dysfunction ... The exact converse applies to any woman.
>
> (Masters & Johnson, 1970, p. 4)

A second reason for the dual-sex team is related to transference. On the one hand, the dual team serves to minimize unproductive transference while, on the other hand, it enhances useful transference. Because the primary relationship in sex therapy is between the partners and not so much between the clients and therapists (as is usually the case in individual therapy), Masters and Johnson discovered that a dual-sex therapy team reduced unproductive and distracting transference by de-emphasizing the therapist–client interaction. The perception that clients tend to have with dual-sex therapy teams, that they "each [have] a friend in court as well as an interpreter when participating in the [treatment] program" (Masters & Johnson, 1970, p. 4), promotes positive transference.

Additionally, because sex therapy can present ethical and even legal concerns, the dual-sex therapy team creates a therapeutic environment that provides protection and aids a useful transference such that the therapists are viewed only in terms of the limited professional roles of medical and psychological authorities.

Although clinicians originally heralded the dual therapist team approach as "an extremely exciting research and clinical breakthrough in sexual knowledge," they also pointed out that "there are some evident problems in applying this model to 'typical' therapeutic practice," not least of which is the "much greater time commitment on the part of two therapists" (McCarthy, 1973, p. 290). Most therapists do not have the luxury of dual-sex teams, and this clinical model has been adapted to single therapist, outpatient settings.

> It would appear that as long as the therapist is aware of both male and female physical and psychological responses, as well as the power and communication aspects of the triadic therapeutic relationship, then he or she can function in a therapeutic way.
>
> (McCarthy, 1973, p. 293)

Modifications for Diverse Populations

For Specific Sexual Dysfunctions

In presenting the specific sexual dysfunctions, we will in general follow the sexual dysfunction categorization scheme offered by *DSM-5*. In this scheme, all of the sexual dysfunctions subsequently described will meet the following criteria to be diagnostically significant:

1. They occur 75–100% of the time;
2. They must be of at least six months' duration;
3. They must have caused significant distress for one or both partners;
4. They can be described as either lifelong or acquired;
5. They can be identified as situational or generalized; and
6. They can be rated as mild, moderate, or severe.

However, one of the problems with highly controversial diagnostic schemes like the *DSM-5* is that, in our opinion, they have become too medicalized. According to the new criteria, none of the sexual dysfunctions listed meet formal diagnostic criteria according to the *DSM-5* if they are primarily associated with an individual psychological disorder, relationship distress, life stressors, or sociocultural factors. All these are, for the moment, characterized merely as "associated features." In this manual we will, to a much greater degree, emphasize the role that psychosocial factors play in the development and maintenance of sexual concerns than is the case in the Statistical Manual.

We have included a checklist in Appendix C for many of the specific instructions and modifications suggested in the following pages of this chapter.

Male Hypoactive Sexual Desire Disorder
Definition

Male HSDD is a new category in *DSM-5*. It is diagnosed when a man regularly and over time does not experience sexual or arousing thoughts or fantasies and has a lack of desire for sexual activity. Men diagnosed with HSDD may not initiate sexual activity or are generally unreceptive to partner initiation. Masturbation and sexual activity with a partner may take place but only infrequently. Merely having low sexual desire does not suffice for a diagnosis of HSDD because, as with other sexual dysfunctions in the *DSM-5*, the lack of fantasy/interest *must cause distress* to one or both partners. The diagnosis must be made in consideration of the man's age and sociocultural background. It does not simply reflect a difference in level of interest between the man and his partner. This difference in level of interest is more accurately described as *desire discrepancy*. As with other dysfunctions, the problem must persist or be intermittent for six months. A man with a lifelong lack of fantasy and interest but who also identifies as asexual would not be given this diagnosis.

Prevalence

Until recently, Male HSSD was considered rare and few men presented with it for sex therapy. But now studies suggest that this diagnosis occurs in approximately 15–25% of the male population across the lifespan and is particularly common in older men. As many as 41% of men aged 66–74 years experience HSDD. Besides age, the other factors that must be considered when working with HSDD are general health, the difference between sexual interest and sexual desire, the degree to which the individual or partner experiences distress in response to the level of desire, and the duration of the problem. Perhaps reflecting cultural or religious factors such as inhibitions and prohibitions against sexual activity, the *DSM-5* reports that while 12.5% of men of Northern European descent report low desire, 28% of men 40–80 years of age, of Southeast Asian descent, report it.

Presentation
Cases of HSDD usually fall into one of four categories:

(1) HSDD with significant biomedical involvement;
(2) HSDD without biomedical involvement;
(3) lack of desire for sex with a current partner – sexual desire is being fulfilled otherwise; and
(4) lack of desire for sex with a current partner – sexual desire is being suppressed.

(Meana & Steiner, 2014, p. 49)

Etiology and Assessment
In order to accurately assess these four, the clinician must take a detailed history of the client's medical situation, including the medications he is taking, alcohol use or abuse, and the use of illicit drugs. Medical conditions that involve the kidneys, cardiovascular system, central nervous system, and a history of cancer must be evaluated. Most important, however, is a consideration of the endocrine system, especially whether there is a presence of hypogonadism, hyperprolactinemia, thyroid disorders, and diabetes. All of these conditions may affect the level of testosterone in the blood stream that, in turn, may affect the level of a man's desire. However, except in cases of hypogonadal disorder, the role of testosterone in male desire is not entirely clear: "There … may be a critical threshold below which testosterone will affect sexual desire in men and above which there is little effect of testosterone on men's desire" (*DSM-5*) (American Psychiatric Association, 2015, p. 442).

There is another source of HSDD that is often overlooked and to which Meana and Steiner (2014) refer as the "hidden" contributors. These include a past history of erection concerns about which the HSDD client may not be entirely aware, or may be unwilling to share early in the Sensate Focus process. Additionally, it is important to assess the role of a history of ejaculatory problems (either early or delayed). Clients may have developed a protective, secondary, and presenting complaint of lack of desire. This is often associated with repression of sexual fantasy in response to, and as a deflection away from, these earlier sexual difficulties about which the client may be uncomfortable. When clients are uncomfortable discussing the erectile or ejaculatory history hidden behind the HSDD, sometimes an individual assessment session, as opposed to a conjoint session, may help tease this out. Alternatively, sometimes when clients are uncomfortable discussing their erectile or ejaculatory history underlying the HSDD, the opposite is true: a conjoint history-taking session or a history-taking session with the other partner alone, may be much more helpful as the partner is more likely to provide accurate information about this hidden contributor. This is an example of why taking both an individual history as well as the history of the partner is so critical. It is important for sex therapists to be aware of these potentially hidden factors during both the sex history and also during the processing of Sensate Focus sessions. As noted, Sensate Focus itself can be a powerful diagnostic procedure, revealing underlying contributors to sexual difficulties that clients are unprepared to reveal during the sex history.

In our experience, most of the other factors associated with Male HSDD do not easily fit in the formal *DSM-5* criteria for diagnosis. Among the most important are partner and relationship factors. These include the build-up of anger and resentment over: perceived partner criticism; power struggles; partner's sexual issues; and partner's health limitations, among other issues. These also include determining whether the HSDD client is fulfilling needs for sexual release by means other than those involving his partner. This may include masturbation, pornography, extra-relationship affairs, or alternative sexual interests. Additionally, assessing the partner's attraction for the HSDD client is critical. However, when the HSDD client attributes his dysfunction to factors such as "My partner has gained weight," it is important for the clinician to consider the possibility that this is not the primary issue. Instead, it may be a more culturally acceptable way for the client to explain his lack of interest.

The HSDD client must also be evaluated for individual psychological factors such as depression, anxiety, childhood neglect, or emotional or sexual trauma. These men have a higher incidence of depression and anxiety. They may also be experiencing reactions to changes in sexual responsiveness due to age or resulting from medical procedures such as prostate surgery.

Environmental stressors impacting the HSDD client, as well as his partner, may include job loss, family concerns, bereavement, or workaholism. Cultural or religious factors such as inhibitions and prohibitions against sexual activity need to be examined. Men with HSDD often come from backgrounds where emphasis was placed on both emotional restraint and also on the negative aspects of sexual expression, often contributing to a deep sense of shame about sexuality.

Specific Treatment Modifications of Sensate Focus for Male Hypoactive
Sexual Desire Disorder

Clinicians are much more likely to regard female clients as susceptible to low sexual desire and may overlook the significance of the changes necessary to work with HSDD men. Presuming that the medical and health contributors, if any, have been eliminated or adequately addressed, Sensate Focus with HSDD men begins with readjusting their expectations.

Individual Sessions

Either to help with the educational process or simply because of the HSDD man's anxieties about his sexual appetite, he may respond best to having some individual sessions prior to or together with couple's Sensate Focus. This is particularly true when the richness of the client's fantasy life is in question. Many HSDD clients feel ashamed of the fact that they perceive themselves as less masculine because of their limited fantasy life, and they may need education and support for this issue. It is important to remember that even though expectations are that men know what stimulates them, any particular male client may not necessarily be aware of this.

In initial sessions, self-Sensate Focus opportunities may be suggested. During these, the HSDD client is guided to focus on the sensations provided by his own body. He begins touching himself mindfully from head to toe, avoiding at first any areas of his body that represent something sexual for him. Eventually he will include these areas into his self-touch.

Fantasies and Visual Sensations

If the client is not channeling sexual tension away from the relationship by fantasizing, or by reading or watching erotic material in order to fantasize, or by zeroing in on the visual sensations he might find stimulating, he may actually be encouraged to cultivate these as means for enhancing his sensorial involvement. He is urged to spend between 10 and 15 minutes a day, six days a week, recollecting or creating imagined scenarios, or using visual or written materials he thinks once were, or might become, stimulating. This, of course, presumes that he and the partner are both agreeable. The emphasis, as with couple Sensate Focus, is on his sensory experience in the moment, without judgment or expectation. Every time he finds himself distracted by demanding thoughts, he refocuses on sensations in the moment.

It is important to make a comment here about visual sensations. Since visual sensations provide many men with additional gateways into arousal, encouraging men with HSDD to consciously attend to these may be helpful. Just as with touch sensations, many people are not aware of the different categories of visual sensations. While touch sensations may be defined as temperature, pressure, and texture, visual sensations include *color*, *shape*, *shading* (dark or light), and the combination of these three to suggest *movement*. Making these dimensions concrete can be of great assistance not only to men with HSDD but to men experiencing other sexual dysfunctions as well.

However, while cultivating his sensory and imaginal repertoire, the man with HSDD is discouraged from masturbating to orgasm to this fantasy or visual material unless he has an extremely limited fantasy life, or such limited awareness of what absorbs him sensorally, that doing so would be therapeutic. If the client has never or rarely masturbated, he may need support for self-Sensate Focus before he engages with his partner. This may involve mindfully focusing on tactile or other sensory experience that helps focus him on his physicality. It may include the use of fabrics he finds absorbing, or vibrator stimulation to intensify the sensations.

Education About the Cultural Portrayal of Men

Whether done in individual sessions or sessions with the partner, it is important to educate HSDD clients about the unrealistic portrayals of male sexual prowess in movies and especially in pornography. Men are not always ready for sex, at "the drop of a bra" as William Masters was fond of saying or, as we have experienced with Gay men, at "the sight of a crotch." The waxing and waning of sexual desire must be normalized. As with all clients, they must also be offered support and hope that their concerns can be addressed.

Spontaneity

Educating the HSDD man about over-valuing spontaneity is another important consideration. With these clients, almost more than any other, it is critical to inform them how unrealistic it is to expect that spontaneous sexual interest will occur in the context and daily routine of a long-term committed relationship.

Modifications for Diverse Populations

Couple Sessions

When couple's Sensate Focus is initiated, HSDD men are encouraged to participate on a regular basis with no more than 72 hours (preferably 48 hours) separating the opportunities. Frequency is emphasized over the length of individual sessions; it is the regularity of contact that is most important for building sexual tension. Scheduling the sessions is frequently helpful because often clients who experience HSDD may be more controlled, structured individuals and they respond well to planning ahead. Scheduling the sessions can also alleviate the problems associated with relegating touching to times when energy is likely to be lowest, for example, late at night.

It is often important to have the HSDD client initiate the Sensate Focus sessions at least in the beginning of treatment. This is also diagnostic because if he does not initiate there is much grist for the therapeutic mill in terms of the resistances he is experiencing, and how to manage them.

Additionally, scheduling sessions can assist with problematic relationship dynamics. It can ease timing problems associated with pressured physical contact in response to the partner's frustrations over not having had sexual contact for a long period of time. "One partner insists on having his or her 'needs' met, and the other reacts to this insistence by withdrawing. The more the latter withdraws, the more the former demands, and vice versa" (Meana & Steiner, 2014, p. 52). This dynamic may show up in Sensate Focus as it did in their previous attempts to address the problem.

Another relationship concern is the man's feeling empowered to have greater control over not only the timing of, but also the specific activities associated with, Sensate Focus. Many men with HSDD experience themselves as having little input into the sensual contact they have with their partners, or are concerned that the input they would like to have will not be well received. For example, one client reported that he would like to have some coverings over the lamps in the room during the Sensate Focus sessions. This might seem like a little detail; however, not only did it mean a lot to him in terms of feeling more empowered but also he had never shared this with his partner. It opened the floodgates for many more conversations about their sensual interchange.

If, either through the history-taking or the Sensate Focus sessions, it becomes apparent that a major source of the client's difficulties is concern about ejaculatory control or erection response, the changes that are suggested below in the sections on Premature Ejaculation and Erection Disorders can be incorporated into the Sensate Focus activities for the HSDD client. Actually, the emphasis is on treating the primary etiological factor, namely, the Early/Delayed Ejaculation or the Erection Disorder, and then the avoidance of sexual contact evidenced by the HSDD client will likely decrease.

Female Sexual Interest/Arousal Disorder

Definition

Female Sexual Interest/Arousal Disorder (FSIAD) is a new composite *DSM-5* category that combines the previous diagnoses of Hypoactive Sexual Desire Disorder and Female Sexual Arousal Disorder from the *Diagnostic and Statistical Manual of Mental Disorders-IV* (*DSM-IV-TR*) (American Psychiatric Association, 2003). This change was made, in part, because research indicates that *desire may follow rather than precede sexual activity for a number of women* (Basson, 2002a; Basson, 2002b; Carvalheira, Brotto, & Leal, 2010).

Women diagnosed with FSIAD must meet three of the following six criteria:

1. Interest in sexual activity fails to emerge during a sexual encounter;
2. There are reduced, or there is an absence of, fantasy, sexual or erotic thoughts;
3. There is a lack of initiation or reduced initiation or receptivity to sexual activity;
4. The woman experiences reduced pleasure or sexual excitement during sexual activity;
5. There is an absence of or reduced sexual interest/arousal in response to sexual cues (e.g., written, verbal, visual, etc.); and/or
6. There is a reduction in or absence of genital or other sexual sensations.

Despite the fact that, by definition, sexual dysfunctions must result in distress for one or both partners, there is little emphasis in the publications on FSIAD about this characteristic when it comes to the female client (Brotto & Luria, 2014). However, it has been our experience that for treatment to be successful the woman, herself, must ultimately claim her own interest in treatment for herself, not simply to avoid relationship distress.

Prevalence

Lack of sexual desire is the most common and distressing sexual complaint of women, particularly, but not exclusively, of younger women. However, since FSIAD is a new diagnosis, there are few studies that suggest its prevalence. Preliminary results hint that anywhere from 10.2 to 40.6% of women aged 16–44 experience problems with sexual interest or desire, depending on whether it is measured as existing from one month or six months (Mercer et al., 2003).

Presentation

FSIAD clients may seek help as a result of partner pressure or because they, themselves, are distressed about their lack of interest. Brotto and Luria suggest that FSIAD presents in three major ways: "I've lost my libido," or women who have difficulty becoming interested before or during sex but would like to regain their desire; "It takes a long time for me to get sexually excited," or women who do not experience desire before physical contact but who, after some longer-than-preferred amount of time, are able to become aroused; and "I would be content if we never had sex again!" or women who are not interested before or during sex, and who have little interest in regaining their desire (Brotto & Luria, 2014, p. 18). Women in this last category are often encouraged to come to therapy by their partners.

Etiology and Assessment

As with Male HSDD, it is critical to take a detailed history of the client's medical situation. Conditions that are believed to affect desire and arousal in women are circulatory, musculoskeletal, central nervous, and endocrinological, including low estrogen and testosterone levels. However, the specific nature of these effects is complex and confusing. For example, with regard to endocrine considerations,

> In a number of studies ... a weak correlation between lower levels of estradiol and decreased sexual desire has been found by some ... but not by others ... Despite

long-held popular beliefs, population-based studies have shown minimal or no correlation between testosterone levels and sexual desire in women.

(Brotto & Luria, 2014, pp. 24–25)

Nonetheless, all of these systemic concerns should be considered.

In our clinical experience, the pairing of lack of sexual interest with lack of physiological response is rare except in cases that are hormonal, that result from clinical
depression and/or anxiety, or that are a response to medication or a medical condition.
A medical factor, such as having radiation, chemotherapy, or removal of her uterus, can
obviously have an impact on a woman and not just from the medical procedure itself. For
some, these may have significant sexual, psychological, and relationship effects in addition to anything physical that results. This has to be acknowledged and Sensate Focus
needs to be reframed in terms of what can now be done rather than what was previously
possible.

Somewhat more common in our experience than the pairing of the lack of sexual interest with the lack of physiological response in the absence of a medical issue is reduced or
modified pleasure in sexual response, and the perception that there is an absence of sexual
response to effective stimulation. The first reflects the importance of looking at relationship
dynamics. More important than hormonal issues for most women are their feelings about
their partner and the relationship. For example, a woman who might report a reduced or modified experience of sexual pleasure paired with loss of desire may be one who has repeatedly
had sexual relations with a partner to avoid or resolve tension in the relationship (something
we refer to as *service organization sex*), leading to feelings of resentment. Clearly, conflictual
relationship dynamics like these may have negative effects on sexual desire and responsivity.
Relationship difficulties that threaten security and fidelity need to be evaluated. Ironically, as
Esther Perel (2007) has reminded us, one of the main contributors to a loss in sexual interest
and arousal can be an excess of security and familiarity; the very ingredients that go into
making a relationship erotic in the beginning (novelty, unpredictability) may erode as the
realities of what makes a long-term relationship work (stability and commitment) become
evident.

The absence of sexual response to effective sexual stimulation often suggests the importance of exploring sociocultural issues. For example, the partner of an FSIAD client may see
the woman's sexual response (nipple erection, areola swelling, lubrication, sex flush, rhythmic
vaginal contractions, etc.) while the woman, herself, remains unaware of her own reactions.
The results of a study by Chivers and Daily (2005) is interesting in this regard. Both men and
women were shown six videos of both human and non human sexual activity. The women
were found to be physiologically aroused to all 6 vignettes as measured by blood flow to the
genitals but they did not necessarily report subjective arousal. It was theorized that one reason
was that subjects repressed their awareness of their own physiological arousal, or were unwilling to report it, as a result of sociocultural pressures not to be aroused to certain sexual stimuli.
It comes as no surprise that these sociocultural factors have a significant impact on sexuality
in general, and its development and expression in women in particular. The results of a study
by Robbins et al. (2011) suggest that while 62.6% of 14-year-old boys and 80% of 17-year-old

boys masturbate, only 43.3% of 14-year-old girls and 58% of 17-year-old girls engage in self-stimulation.

Another, more biological interpretation is that the physiological response to sexual stimulation may be a physical protective mechanism to avoid trauma to the body during rape.

Yet another factor to explore for women who are unaware of or unwilling to report observable arousal comes from a trauma-informed perspective. A sexual trauma survivor who experiences or suppresses physiological arousal during sexual assault or abuse may develop dissociation or repress awareness of their current responses in order to defend against shame or guilt.

The influence of cultural norms on FSIAD women is no more apparent than in the negative images these clients so often have about their bodies. The relation between negative body image and low sexual desire is well documented. The perceived failure to achieve socially approved standards for physical attractiveness is regarded as one of the two most powerful psychological contributors to hypoactive desire disorder in women. This highlights the significance of evaluating both sociocultural and psychological factors.

The other most common factor contributing to FSIAD has to do with environmental stressors: many FSIAD women are overwhelmed by myriad responsibilities they have fulfilling their professional, domestic, relationship, and social roles. They are often either mentally or physically exhausted, or both. Research on women working at home, women working both at home and at a job, and women working both at home and at a career indicated that especially women who are involved in careers while also holding down the fort at home are much more likely to experience decreased sexual desire (Avery-Clark, 1986). It is difficult to feel sexually interested or aroused, or even be aware of these even if they are present, when you are so preoccupied with obligations that you have no time to pay attention to these experiences.

Specific Treatment Modifications of Sensate Focus for Female Sexual Interest/Arousal Disorder

Despite being an advocate of sexual science, when it comes to FSIAD, Kathryn Hall suggests that it may be the case that, as yet, "Sexual medicine has little to offer women in terms of enhancing their sexual desire and pleasure" (2016, p. 390). Therapy usually moves quickly to psychological and relational interventions.

In cases in which the woman is not experiencing personal distress by her lower interest or arousal, and is coming to therapy as the result of partner pressure, the first treatment concern is to assist the woman with finding her own motivation for working on the issue. Without this, treatment success is highly questionable.

Individual Sessions

We must remember that some women have never or rarely spent time exploring their bodies, cultivating fantasies, and learning what is of interest and arousing to them. The purpose of Sensate Focus with FSIAD women is to help with all these issues. Sensate Focus strategies with these clients usually involve the women either exploring their bodies alone at first in terms of what absorbs their attention, or involving the partner in the exploration. If clients choose to do the touching by themselves, self-Sensate Focus involves mindfully connecting to tactile or other sensory experiences to help ground them in their physicality. It may also include sensory-oriented baths, massages, vibrator stimulation, and physical exercise. Clients are offered sexual information and suggestions for focusing on the sensations provided by their bodies as they begin touching themselves from head to toe as best they can, but avoiding breasts and genitals at first. Eventually clients include their breasts and genitals into the touch. They are encouraged to have one session a day, six days a week, for approximately 10–20 minutes. The emphasis, as with couple's Sensate Focus, is on the physical, sensory experience in the moment, without judgment or expectation, and refocusing from distractions onto the touch sensations.

Fantasies

The development of a rich source of sexual fantasies is another Sensate Focus adjunct with FSIAD clients. Using any literature from romance novels to poetry, and experimenting with visual images, the woman is encouraged to spend some time daily focusing on this part of herself. While men often devote a considerable amount of time in their adolescence and early adulthood to cultivating their interests and fantasies (often paired with self-stimulation), women are less likely to do this. In fact, they may be discouraged from exploring what they find physically and imaginally absorbing especially when their sociocultural or religious family of origin is conservative.

Couple Sessions

Sensate Focus is initiated following or along with self-discovery and fantasy enrichment. The woman moves her partner's hand away if anything is uncomfortable, and uses positive handriding to practice communicating what she might like to explore in that moment. It is important to have the couple slow down so that they can educate themselves and each other about what may be absorbing and ultimately, in Sensate Focus 2, stimulating.

When the couple's Sensate Focus is initiated, and depending on the individual and/or partner dynamics, the client with FSIAD is usually the initiator of the Sensate Focus touching sessions. This is especially the case if she is the member of the couple who has engaged in sexual activity mainly to service her partner. Although the goal is to have the FSIAD client eventually alternate with the partner when it comes to initiating the Sensate Focus sessions, this does not have to be the case at the beginning of Sensate Focus. This is because the FSIAD client may need a number of sessions before she can feel the empowerment of initiating, touching and being for her own interest. A helpful analogy is suggesting that just because one partner is hungry does not mean that both must have a full course meal. All that each partner owes the other is to sit down to the table of the Sensate Focus exercises.

Either the FSIAD partner may decide to stop the session after her portion of the touching has been completed, or she may decline to engage in Sensate Focus at the other person's initiation. This allows her greater comfort and practice when being touched and touching for her own interest. However, she is then to re-initiate that same session at her own behest at some later point. Both partners, but particularly the FSIAD partner, respond best to the suggestions if they have the option of declining or stopping any particular Sensate Focus opportunity. In these cases it is important for the therapist to help the woman pace her initiation and involvement instead of the partner being the one to do this.

Erectile Disorder

Definition

Erectile Disorder (ED) is defined as the regular and repeated inability to achieve or maintain erections that are firm enough for insertion during partnered sexual encounters. A diagnosis must meet one of the following three criteria:

1. A notable difficulty obtaining an erection;
2. A distinct difficulty maintaining an erection once it has been obtained; and/or
3. A marked decrease in the firmness or rigidity of the erection.

The diagnosis is not given if erection concerns are occasional or if they do not create distress for one or both partners in a relationship. As with all other sexual dysfunctions, the erectile concern cannot be more appropriately traced to a different sexual dysfunction (e.g., secondary to Rapid Ejaculation), and it cannot be only the result of factors such as substance abuse or prescribed medications.

Prevalence

ED is present in approximately 10% of men under 35 years of age, and can occur in as many as 50% or more of men over the age of 60. It is susceptible to age and to medical and psychological factors.

Presentation

ED can be generalized or it can also be situational, occurring only with a particular partner, with certain types of partners, in long-term relationships but not in short-term interactions, in certain environments, and under the influence of certain kinds of stressors. A common presentation is men who can have erections with self, partner, or oral stimulation but who lose it at insertion or immediately thereafter. This is especially true in men who experience an erection and attempt to use it immediately over concerns for its loss. ED may also be associated with a previous history or another sexual issue, most often an ejaculatory, problem.

Etiology and Assessment

Erectile Disorders may be primarily biomedical or psychogenic in nature. Often there is significant interaction. Even if medical factors are the initial cause, the individual's psychological confidence and his relationship are sometimes so negatively affected as to contribute further to the disorder and even maintain it autonomously. As mentioned, factors contributing to ED vary, and a multidisciplinary evaluation is critical (Metz & McCarthy, 2004). Both individual self-report and partner observations are taken into consideration. Other physiological procedures such as nocturnal penile tumescence and rigidity measures may be helpful but are used much less frequently than prescribed medication.

In medical terms, ED is not only especially affected by cardiovascular difficulties (hypertension, hypercholesterolemia) but can actually be an early indicator in younger men of impending cardiovascular problems (Rosen, Miner and Wincze, 2014). Other medical factors include endocrine (diabetes, low testosterone, hypothalamic-pituitary-gonadal axis disturbances) and lower urinary tract problems.

Modifications for Diverse Populations

As with Male HSDD, there may be a hidden, or primary, sexual cause of ED that is not at first reported. Research has shown that a history of some other sexual dysfunction may be associated with as many as one-third of cases of erectile insecurity. Particularly in older men, a history or the presence of delayed or absent ejaculation may contribute.

The psychological status of any man presenting for treatment of ED should be evaluated. Important factors include the degree to which the client is affected by performance anxiety associated with concerns about erections, and spectatoring that involves observing the state of engorgement. These are the two most common psychological factors. They are the two distracting thought patterns that make it difficult to focus on sensory absorption during sexual interaction.

Both the man's and the partner's level of knowledge about erections needs to be assessed. While many people have a sophisticated understanding of the physiology and response patterns of male arousal, many do not, and no assumptions should be made about the extent of their knowledge on the subject. For example, few people are aware that the erection response, even in fully functioning men, regularly comes and goes over a period of time. In the absence of fears of performance and spectatoring that result in anxiety, penile engorgement will return at its own natural rate and rhythm.

Men who have experienced sexual abuse are susceptible to ED. This may be the direct result of the abuse itself. Or it may be the result of the intense shame often experienced by men in a culture that recognizes the possibility of women being sexually abused but that places a special stigma on men being the subject of abuse.

The relationship of any man presenting with ED should be evaluated. Interpersonal factors may include hostility between partners. Partner factors may include the experience of pain with intercourse. Others factors include the willingness, or lack thereof, of either the partner or the man himself to incorporate oral or manual stimulation into the physical interactions. The possibility of sexual variation, including oral and manual stimulation, removes pressure from intercourse as a necessity. Determining the partner's level of cooperation with variation can be critical. Additional partner dynamics might be an inhibited partner who will only engage in sexual interactions with the lights off when visual stimulation may be critical for the man especially if he is older.

The degree to which the man with ED may be experiencing gender identity or sexual orientation concerns also needs to be evaluated. This may reflect sociocultural influences. Some men may have entered into traditional marriage and family situations as a result of social pressures when, in fact, they are not comfortable with the gender identification or sexual orientation they present to others. Other cultural and religious factors include a history of negative messages about sexual expression that contribute to shame and guilt. Although body image is often considered when taking the history of a female client, it should not be ignored when evaluating men with ED. Cultural pressures on men to adhere to certain standards of appearance are becoming nearly as intense as those experienced by women. Gay men have been confronting these pressures for a long time, but heterosexual men are increasingly subjected to them as well.

Additionally, situational stressors encountered through work, relationship, and home life should not be neglected in the assessment, and neither should lifestyle patterns associated with alcohol, prescription and street drugs, smoking, exercise, and obesity.

Specific Treatment Modifications of Sensate Focus for Erectile Disorder

The effects of ED may be devastating for the individual as well as for his partner. Clients often come in for therapy feeling very discouraged. Many have already tried medications that worked initially but less so over time. It is important to begin Sensate Focus as quickly as possible in most of these cases.

Medications

Sensate Focus treatment strategies for men with ED follow the usual prescribed hierarchy with the following changes. Depending on the client and partner, some sex therapists will begin treatment with the addition or maintenance of PDE-5 inhibitors such as sildenafil (Viagra), tadalafil (Cialis) and vardenafil (Levitra), eventually discontinuing it as clients experience spontaneous erections with their partners and increased confidence. With the build-up of sexual tension engendered with Sensate Focus, these spontaneous erections, especially morning erections, are reassuring and signal the degree to which anxiety and pressure have been factors in the erectile difficulties.

Couple Sessions

When the couple begins Sensate Focus with breasts, chest, and genitals on limits, the partner is guided to move away from the penis when it becomes engorged. The partner may move to touching other parts of the body, then return regularly to genital touch, and then move away again. This redirects the focus of attention away from engorgement and onto a more full-bodied approach.

During the Sensate Focus sessions, it is not uncommon for a man who has been experiencing satisfactory engorgement with breast and genital touching to experience difficulty when partner astride, genital-to-genital is suggested. To manage this it is important for the therapist to explicitly state that no engorgement is needed for this exercise and that focus is to remain on tactile sensations. However, due to cultural expectations ("I should have an erection!") and the concomitant anxiety, many men either lose engorgement or do not experience engorgement during the initial stages of this exercise. When the partner is playing with his or her genitals against those of the man with ED, the partner may experience a burst of arousal and even be orgasmic, despite the ED client's non-engorged penis. The effect of actually experiencing that engorgement is not essential for the partner's sexual response cannot be underestimated. It does much to dispel the ED client's performance anxiety.

Another suggestion that can help allay the participant's performance apprehension is having the partner do the inserting when the time becomes appropriate. The client with ED is instructed to leave the inserting to his partner, maintaining his focus on the tactile sensations. The client's partner is in a much better position to gauge the firmness of the client's engorgement, gauge when she (or he) is ready for insertion, and knows where the penis goes.

Expanding the Sensory Experience

Another modification for men with ED is to encourage refocusing their visual attention on some aspect of their partner's body they find interesting. As noted in the section on *Specific Treatment Modifications* of Sensate Focus for Male *HSDD*, it can be helpful to encourage the client to expand his sensation repertoire by focusing on the shape, shading, color, and motion offered by visual sensations. When experiencing penile spectatoring the ED man might attend to the shape of the swell of his partner's breasts, or on different tints of the partner's skin. Alternatively, the ED partner may be encouraged to focus on visual imagery in the form of a fantasy if this is within the couple's sexual value system.

Code Word

Most couples grappling with ED are familiar with the experience of sensing when the ED partner is experiencing increasing performance anxiety. Often this results in stopping the touching, mechanically going through the motions of the touching, or falling into a goal-oriented, demanding mindset of working deliberately at it. In order to manage this, couples are encouraged to agree on a positive *code word* that is verbalized by the man when he experiences a rise in anxiety. When he says the code word, both partners change their positions and actions while continuing to touch. This suggestion gives both partners something different to do to override their pattern of helplessness and discouragement in the face of anxiety associated with absent erection or diminished engorgement.

Understanding Erection Responses

As suggested in the ED assessment section, many people are not aware that erection responses ebb and flow even in the most functional men. It can be helpful to both partners to provide information about the fact that, in the absence of anxiety about whether or not an erection will occur or be maintained, penile engorgement will return according to its own natural rate and rhythm.

Paradoxical Injunction

An additional technique that drives home this understanding about how erection responses wax and wane naturally is to suggest that the ED client gain and lose engorgement *on purpose* in the presence of his partner. This can be done before and/or during insertion. If this is done during insertion, the partners remain quiet and intentionally allow the engorgement to diminish. These experiences serve as a paradox: the very thing that is feared is assigned and, since sexual responsiveness is a natural function, conscious attempts to prevent it are more likely to produce it, at least in time. In younger men, this *quiet insertion* with loss of engorgement may take some time to accomplish. Once partners know the erection will return, the anxiety associated with fears of losing the erection will decrease.

Female Orgasmic Disorder

Definition

Female Orgasmic Disorder (FOD) is the inability to experience an orgasm in most, if not all, sexual opportunities. It is also defined as experiencing a reduced intensity of orgasmic sensation in most, if not all, sexual opportunities. This reduced intensity of sensation is new in *DSM-5* and reinforces the fact that orgasm is not an all or nothing experience for women. The new diagnostic criteria include both physiological alterations AND the subjective experience of intensity. This is because, unlike male orgasm, female orgasm has no externally irrefutable signal.

Although approximately 6–15% of women who experience orgasmic difficulties report achieving orgasm too quickly, this is not included under the *DSM-5* classification system for FOD.

Even more so than with FSIAD, publications on FOD frequently fail to emphasize women's own experience of orgasmic concern, or lack thereof, in the diagnosis of the dysfunction. However, as the prevalence statistics below indicate, women, themselves, are often not particularly distressed by what others may label as their orgasmic difficulties.

Prevalence

Depending on which research you examine, FOD impacts between 3 and 41.2% of women. The fact that only between 3.4 and 14.4% of these women report their low or absent orgasmic response as distressing suggests the need for further clarification. FOD appears to be the second most common sexual dysfunction presented by women after FSIAD.

Presentation

Lack of orgasmic release can be a lifelong problem or a recent one. It can be a generalized condition, or related to certain types of stimulation, circumstances, or partners. For example, some women have never achieved an orgasm by any means with self or partner although they may have done so in their sleep state (*somnus orgasm*). However, for the majority of women with this concern, masturbating to orgasm is not a problem when using finger stimulation of the clitoris, rubbing against the bed or another object, squeezing the legs together rhythmically, or using imagery or toys such as dildos and vibrators. Many women, especially younger ones with less partner experience, may seek help for having orgasms when their partner is involved. Some are able to be orgasmic with oral or other stimulation with a partner, but not with insertion, and they hope to experience an orgasm with intercourse.

Menopausal women report somewhat greater difficulty achieving orgasm. They discover the changes occurring with aging, such as vaginal dryness and atrophy causing pain, may preclude insertion or diminish their responsiveness.

The experience of orgasm is extremely variable from woman to woman and differs in intensity for the same woman from occasion to occasion. What we know is that most women require stimulation of the clitoris to be orgasmic with or without intercourse. There is no single approach to orgasmic release that suits all women all the time.

Etiology and Assessment

Most often, orgasmic difficulties are the result of a number of factors, and the focus is on working with more than one of them. Therefore, a multifactorial evaluation is necessary. Medications, including some cancer medications and many of the anti-depressants, may be culprits. Between 30 and 60% of women on these medications are orgasmically affected by them (Montgomery, Baldwin, & Riley, 2002). Other medical variables impacting orgasmic release include radiation treatment, spinal nerve damage, chronic or progressive medical conditions (thyroid conditions, diabetes, multiple sclerosis), and include surgeries (e.g., pelvic nerve damage from radical hysterectomy). In the case of women who have hysterectomies,

Modifications for Diverse Populations

some of them may have previously focused on contractions of the cervix or uterus and, if so, they may report a diminished or absent orgasmic response.

Orgasmic difficulty may be influenced by psychological and learning factors as well. One of the most important ones to assess is the specific manner in which the woman has attempted to bring herself to orgasm in the past. Detailed information is critical because individual preferences vary tremendously. Additional factors for consideration may include:

1. General sexual inhibition;
2. Low self-esteem;
3. Lack of familiarity with one's body;
4. Serious concerns about one's body and its appearance;
5. Anxiety or depression;
6. Fear of loss of control or vulnerability;
7. Personality factors (e.g., introversion, inhibition, emotional dysregulation, hesitation in engaging in new experiences);
8. A history of neglect, or emotional, physical or sexual abuse; and
9. Pregnancy concerns.

For many women, the inability to shift out of the analytic, task-oriented mindset that is useful for meeting responsibilities, and into the sensorially-oriented experiential mindset is a major factor. When clinically significant mental illness appears to be the primary cause of orgasmic dysfunction, a DSM diagnosis of FOD is not made.

Other individual contributions to FOD that are in need of evaluation include the extent to which the woman has cultivated her subjective experience of sexuality and her comfort level with this. For example, many women with orgasmic and other sexual difficulties do not allow themselves to fantasize or even think about sex very often. They infrequently engage themselves in any form of sensual appreciation. When they are involved in sex, they may also try to consciously make orgasm happen which only makes it less likely to occur.

Partner factors may also be relevant. These include partner health status, concomitant sexual problems (e.g., rapid ejaculation), or poor partner technique. The latter may dovetail with relationship factors that also need to be explored, such as poor non-verbal or verbal skills between the partners. However, current research suggests that it "is not clear whether the communication problems were a cause or an effect of the orgasmic difficulties" (Graham, 2014, p. 98).

A variety of other relationship variables may require assessment. Lack of quality time, lack of privacy, and lack of general relationship skills (e.g., conflict resolution), power inequities and the associated build-up of resentments, and discrepancies in sexual interest that may have contributed to one partner's pressuring the other for sex and/or orgasm, may all be factors in FOD. Severe relationship distress that includes emotional, sexual, or physical abuse clearly may be related factors.

Sociocultural and religious expectations may also affect sexual responsivity alone and/or with her partner. The manner in which a woman is raised to think about and develop her sexuality can have a tremendous impact on whether she grows up with deeply ingrained barriers to arousal and orgasmic release, or whether she has learned to integrate her sexuality into her growth as a person. For example, because of sociocultural and religious values, some women are highly responsive by themselves but have difficulty being orgasmic with a partner because she is so focused on the partner's experience. Additionally, some women have not been permitted or willing to engage in masturbation. Research suggests that there is a positive correlation between women who masturbate before marriage and their ability to be orgasmic with their partners.

Finally, lifestyle stressors, such as excessive works hours, job loss, care of elderly relatives and young children, and bereavement must be evaluated. These may be powerful influences.

Specific Treatment Modifications of Sensate Focus for Female Orgasmic Disorder
Medications
There are a number of biomedical strategies that may be considered before trying Sensate Focus or while working with these procedures. For example, if the woman is on an SSRI antidepressant or birth control, and if this is suspected to be contributing to the orgasmic difficulties, a change in medication may be helpful. As yet, there are currently no pharmacological medications or treatments for anorgasmic women that have been approved (Graham, 2014). Medications such as sildenafil, estrogen, testosterone, tibolone, and a variety of nutritional supplements have not produced reliable results.

Individual Sessions
Sensate Focus strategies for women who have never achieved orgasm by any means (except in sleep) begin with education about their own bodies through self-touch Sensate Focus exercises. Following procedures developed by Dodson (1996), and Heiman and LoPiccolo (1988), these are initiated with Directed Masturbation (DM) techniques. These include education about orgasmic experience, the use of Kegel exercises to strengthen Pubococcygeal (PC) muscle control, and self-Sensate Focus.

For women who have reduced sensation due to neurologic or medical procedures, medications or illnesses, or for any woman experiencing FOD, the development of fantasy with reading material and visual images can be very helpful. For women who have had a hysterectomy and had focused on the pleasurable sensations of uterine contractions during orgasm, teaching them to refocus on other parts of the body in contraction can be very productive. The intense use of a vibrator can be valuable, particularly if the more powerful type is incorporated into the touching. Unfortunately, apparatuses, such as the Eros clitoral therapy device, have not shown to be consistently effective with anorgasmic women.

Couple Sessions
Once the woman has learned how to be orgasmic by herself, she works on communicating her new awareness and needs to her partner. Couple Sensate Focus may begin at the same time as self-Sensate Focus or afterwards.

Sensate Focus techniques for women who want to be orgasmic with partner insertion or intercourse often begin with educating both the woman and her partner about the fact that orgasm with intercourse is often the most challenging way for women to become orgasmic with a partner. Many couples are not aware that many women are not regularly or easily orgasmic with insertion only. They usually need additional clitoral stimulation. This often comes as a surprise.

The Sensate Focus techniques themselves involve the woman's learning to receive and give themselves clitoral stimulation at the same time they are exploring pelvic body alignment (the coital alignment technique, or CAT). Here the client focuses on touch sensations while discovering different ways in which she can shift her pelvis to obtain more effective clitoral stimulation. This usually includes manual touch, partner touch, genital-to-genital contact, or by other means. For example, using a smaller vibrator along with insertion may be very helpful.

Longer and more varied pre-Sensate Focus exploration periods, mixed with surprises, can also aid the couple. One of the ways of making the experience more varied is to start and stop intercourse using a varied and teasing approach. There is no eleventh commandment that says once there is insertion, thou shalt not change the activity.

Premature (Early or Rapid) Ejaculation

Definition

Premature, Early, or Rapid Ejaculation (PE) has been defined in the *DSM-5* (2015) as a persistent or recurrent pattern of partnered penetration that results in undesired ejaculation within one minute of insertion in 75% or more of sexual intercourse occurrences. The three criteria are: "(1) a short ejaculatory latency; (2) a lack of perceived self-efficacy or control about the timing of ejaculation; and (3) distress and interpersonal difficulty (related to the ejaculatory dysfunction)" (Althof, 2014, pp. 113–114).

Emphasis is placed not only on the duration until ejaculation but also on the psychosocial impact that PE has on the man, his partner, their sexual relationship, and their relationship in general. While alluding to PE occurring in non-vaginal penetration, the *DSM-5* offers no specific duration criteria.

Prevalence

Self-report investigations suggest that PE affects 20–30% of men. However, since self-report measures do not necessarily meet formal diagnostic standards, the actual prevalence may be somewhat lower, perhaps as low as 1–2%. Although PE has long been considered a dysfunction more common to younger men, recent research suggests that this is not necessarily the case and that it does not necessarily diminish with advancing age.

Presentation

PE may present as either lifelong or acquired. Men who have lifelong PE have always experienced ejaculatory control problems. Men with acquired PE develop ejaculatory control problems following a period of control. Lifelong PE is two times more common than acquired. Some men struggling with lifelong PE may suffer from a biological susceptibility to the dysfunction, the specific physiology of which has yet to be entirely determined.

PE can present as either situational or generalized across partners and situations. Many men will not meet the formal *DSM-5* criteria and may last longer with partnered insertion, but the couple may identify Early Ejaculation as a problem in their sexual relationship because they would like a longer period of intercourse. Some men have no difficulty delaying ejaculation with self-stimulation or with partner manual or oral sex but cannot delay ejaculation with partner insertion.

It is not uncommon for acquired PE to be associated with erectile insecurity, especially in older men. In these cases, PE may result from conditioning that is associated with efforts to ejaculate before the loss of erection. In these cases, erectile insecurity may be the primary difficulty and focus of treatment.

Etiology and Assessment

As with other sexual difficulties, many factors must be evaluated when assessing PE (Metz & McCarthy, 2003). The initial one is whether the dysfunction is lifelong or acquired, because the former is more likely to suggest a biological vulnerability not infrequently associated with serotonin functioning. In these cases, SSRIs (e.g., Prozac and Zoloft) can be helpful, especially in the absence of significant individual and/or relationship difficulties. Other medical factors that occur less often but that are important to consider include genetic predispositions, endo-crinological concerns, increased penile sensitivity associated with nerve transmission disor-ders, and prostatitis. For example, PE may include a complex and as yet poorly understood relationship among depression, serotonin, and thyroid functioning. Althof asserts, "50% of men with hyperthyroidism had PE and, when successfully treated, the prevalence of PE fell to 15%" (2014, p. 118). An additional medical-related issue in need of further study is drug use and particularly withdrawal from opiates.

Psychological factors associated with PE include:

1. Anxious feelings of a phobic, conflictual, or anticipatory nature;
2. Early experiences where importance was placed on ejaculating quickly (e.g., concerns that the parents would come home);
3. Lack of sensory awareness of the level of sexual excitement;
4. Embarrassment about the difficulty;
5. Hostile feelings towards the partner coupled with passive-aggressive expression of this hostility; and
6. Excessive narcissism and an associated lack of concern for partner satisfaction.

Information also needs to be gathered about the man's knowledge of performance anxiety. Although fears of performance aren't usually associated with the original PE experience, they often contribute to the continuation of the problem. Once the man loses his ability to manage his ejaculation, and also loses his sexual confidence in general (about two-thirds of PE men do), this anxiety becomes a distraction from sensory awareness of his level of arousal, and he is even more likely to ejaculate quickly. Once this pattern is in place, the man has little or no voluntary control over his ejaculatory response.

Assessing the partner's awareness of the involuntary nature of the ejaculatory response pattern is also critical. Often the beliefs of the partner that the man with PE can exert control over his ejaculation if he wanted to and if he cared about the partner are sources of partner emotional pain and sexual frustration. Partners may respond with low desire and a lack of willingness to become sexually involved. This is especially the case if there has been no sex-ual release offered by other means or if the partner values having release only with insertion. The lack of ejaculatory control and the partner response may both contribute to the problem. Assessing the partner's willingness to participate in techniques for learning delay is critical.

PE can have a tremendous negative effect on the relationship. These men more often than not avoid sexual interactions with their partners or hesitate to form new sexual relationships.

Modifications for Diverse Populations

They report concerns about their partner's being unfaithful and about lower satisfaction with all aspects of relationship intimacy.

> Women are … angry with their partners with PE because they do not feel that their concerns have been genuinely "heard" by the men nor that they are unwilling to "fix" the problem. Men likewise believe that their partners do not understand the degree of frustration and humiliation that they routinely experience. This disconnection between the men and their partners is the basis for considerable relationship tensions.
>
> (Althof, 2014, p. 121)

In addition to these client and partner issues, it is important to evaluate lifestyle stressors the couple is confronting. For example, hurried sexual interactions are a problem. This may happen when the couple is living with children, relatives, or even a guest, any of whom may knock on the bedroom door at any minute. It would also include long working hours and limited time together, all of which can affect the frequency of intercourse, the amount of time devoted to touching before intercourse, the length of time needed for the man's partner to reach orgasm with insertion as desired, the partners' responses after ejaculation, and the man's awareness of his level of arousal.

Specific Treatment Modifications of Sensate Focus for Early Ejaculation
Medications
Some couples may choose pharmacological intervention, especially several of the SSRIs, prior to or in conjunction with Sensate Focus. These medications are known to delay ejaculation in many men.

Education
Sensate Focus treatment for Early Ejaculation begins with educating clients about the sexual response cycle and the two-stage model of ejaculation: the point of ejaculatory *inevitability* when the man knows he is going to ejaculate but hasn't yet done so; and ejaculation proper when semen is actual expelled.

Individual Sessions: Stop-Start, Squeezes, and more
Clients experiencing PE may be invited initially to practice Sensate Focus sessions while alone, tuning into the tactile sensations. This is instead of returning to their familiar pattern of attempting to delay ejaculation through numbing themselves (e.g., with alcohol) or distracting themselves from the sensations (e.g., using negative imagery). During these self-stimulation sessions they are asked to practice at least one of several ejaculatory control techniques. The first approach is often Seman's Stop-Start Method (1956). Clients are asked to self-stimulate until they can feel their arousal moving up quickly, stop for a few seconds, resume until they can feel their arousal moving up quickly again, stop for a second time, re-stimulate, and then allow themselves to ejaculate on the third or a subsequent opportunity. They are reassured that some loss of engorgement is to be expected but will return with re-stimulation.

Instead of distracting himself with negative imagery, the client is encouraged to do the very opposite, to become ever more attentive to how aroused he is, and to practice stopping well before reaching ejaculatory inevitability. The goal here is twofold. The exercises assist him in reconditioning the ejaculatory response and also teach him to become increasingly aware of his level of arousal. Nonetheless, if the client waits until the point of ejaculatory inevitability to stop, he is invited to appreciate the ejaculation as it occurs instead of trying to stop it at that point (an impossibility). He is then encouraged to continue practicing mindfulness with regard to his arousal and to cease stimulation well before ejaculating.

An additional focus is to encourage him to tune into his PC muscles intermittently to check the degree of tension he is experiencing with anxiety and higher levels of arousal and to practice releasing them. By intentionally squeezing these muscles in a paradoxical fashion, tightening them, and then letting them go, he can check and correct tension being held in the pelvis. He will likely interpret this letting go as relaxation because of the difference between the tension associated with intentionally tightening the PC muscles, and the letting go of this tension. He will further interpret this sense of release (relaxation) as his making progress because no longer will his PC muscles be in the taut state that is indicative of impending orgasm. In order to arrive at a less tense state that counters ejaculation, he is also encouraged to take in a deep breath and release it as he lets go of the tension in his PC.

During the self-stimulation Sensate Focus sessions, clients may be encouraged to try two other types of squeezes. These are referred to as the *Coronal* and the *Basilar* squeezes (see Illustrations 7.1 and 7.2). Although the Coronal Squeeze in particular is the essential squeeze used for treating PE when the partner is also involved, and while it is more effective in this context, both it and the Basilar Squeeze can be initiated during the self-stimulation sessions (Puppo, 2013). It must be initiated at the early stages of self-stimulation and must be applied periodically, approximately every one or two minutes. The use of these two squeezes, both including the partner and by the PE client himself, is described in detail in the next section on *Couple Sessions*. However, when the Coronal Squeeze is used in the individual sessions, the PE client obviously applies the Coronal Squeeze himself rather than having the partner do it, and he uses different finger placements.

As the client reports better latency with manual stimulation, additional suggestions are offered, such as the use of powder, oil, or lotion to create a slicker, more-stimulating surface. A masturbatory sleeve may also be useful for providing a stimulating middle step between self-contact with the hand and insertion with the partner. Masturbatory sleeves are flexible tubes made with one or two openings and an inner surface that feel more like a vagina or anus than does a hand. These can offer clients a chance to practice more with the stop/start technique and also to build additional confidence and control.

Couple Sessions: Stop-Start, Squeezes, and more

The next step may involve incorporating the partner into the treatment. Some sex therapists begin with this couple's phase, including the partner in all parts of treatment. Some therapists emphasize the Coronal and the Basilar squeezes while others focus on the Stop-Start method.

The couple sessions follow the usual Sensate Focus protocol with partners engaging in the my turn/your turn touching with breasts, chest, and genitals off limits. As soon as they move to including the genitals into the contact, and at the moment that the partner has first contact with the PE client's genitals, he or she applies the Coronal Squeeze quickly

7.1
Coronal Squeeze

and very firmly (see Illustration 7.1). The partner does this by placing his or her *thumb on the centerline of the frenulum* on the under side of the penis, and positions the *index and middle fingers directly opposite* the thumb, *just above and below the center line of the coronal ridge*, on the upper side of the penis. The partner applies the squeeze suddenly, with *very* firm pressure, counting silently, "One thousand one, one thousand two, one thousand three," and then releases the squeeze abruptly. It is very important that the fingers are directly opposed to each other down the midline of both the upper side and underside of the penis, and not off on the sides of the penis, and that the squeeze is applied *very* firmly. Otherwise, the PE client may experience the contact as stimulating rather than as interrupting the ejaculatory response.

One of the advantages of implementing the Coronal Squeeze during couple sessions is that the partner's applying it is more effective than when the client applies it himself. This is because of the element of surprise. The nervous system of the man experiencing PE has time to anticipate the squeeze when he is applying it, even if only by a fraction of a second, whereas he does not have time to anticipate it when the partner applies it. Therefore, when the partner applies it, the penile nerves associated with ejaculation are interrupted just that much more abruptly. This speeds up the ejaculatory reconditioning process.

If the Coronal Squeeze is used by the PE client himself during self-Sensate Focus sessions, the man is directed to put his *index and middle fingers on the frenulum* on the under side of the penis and to position his *thumb directly opposite of these, just below the coronal ridge on the upper side*. He also applies the squeeze suddenly, with a *very* firm pressure, counting to himself, "One thousand one, one thousand two, one thousand three," and then releases the squeeze abruptly. He then continues to self-stimulate, applying the squeeze again as before. The Coronal Squeeze reduces the urgency to ejaculate. He then continues to self-stimulate, applying the squeeze again as before.

There is another squeeze that the PE client can apply during both the couple sessions and individual sessions. This is the Basilar Squeeze (see Illustration 7.2). The Basilar Squeeze should be applied only *after* the PE client has achieved some degree of ejaculatory control with the Stop-Start method and the Coronal Squeeze, and/or during the individual, self-Sensate Focus sessions *after* he has obtained some degree of ejaculatory control. When this squeeze is used in the couple sessions, it first involves the partner's wrapping his or her hand around the base of the penis (where it joins the body) and, just as with the Coronal Squeeze, squeezing it very firmly, counting silently for three seconds, and then suddenly releasing. At some point when sufficient ejaculatory control has been achieved, the PE client can take over applying the Basilar Squeeze especially just prior to insertion.

When the Basilar Squeeze is used by the PE client himself during individual sessions, he applies it just as he does with the Coronal Squeeze except in this case at the base of the penis rather than at the coronal ridge. He applies the squeeze suddenly as he feels his level of arousal increasing, counting to himself as he also does with the Coronal Squeeze, and then abruptly releasing.

The Stop-Start method is also very effective when used in the couple sessions with PE clients and their partners. They begin with the partner touching the man with PE while the man directs stopping and starting with both hand stimulation and later the Stop-Start technique with insertion. The couple may use a code word that is said when the man's arousal is increasing, and then both stop moving.

The touching sequence, regardless of whether the Stop-Start, Coronal Squeeze, and/or Basilar Squeeze techniques are applied, then follows the usual hierarchical steps of Sensate Focus. After there has been touching with breasts, chests, and genitals off limits, the next step is having them on limits, then mutual touching, and then partner astride. The partner applies the Coronal Squeeze just prior to insertion and, initially, insertion takes place without movement. If the Basilar Squeeze technique is used, the client squeezes the base of the penis prior to insertion. All of this is accompanied by the Stop-Start technique and the Basilar Squeeze with movement. With heterosexual couples, the partner astride position is recommended because of the greater ejaculatory control it usually provides.

As partners of clients with PE are often frustrated, it is helpful to discuss options for their own release before or after the Sensate Focus suggestions, if they would like. This may include liberally involving the PE client, or partners can provide themselves with release on their own.

7.2
Basilar Squeeze

Delayed Ejaculation

Definition

Delayed Ejaculation (DE) is a condition in which men, even in the presence of sufficient stimulation, find it "difficult or impossible to ejaculate *and* experience orgasm. This diagnosis requires distress about the symptom(s), adequate sexual stimulation, and a conscious desire to achieve orgasm" (Perelman, 2014, p. 139).

Prevalence

Men who have never ejaculated by any means (primary DE) are extremely rare. Men who have acquired delayed ejaculation, especially after age 50, represent perhaps 8–15% of the male population.

Presentation

DE is most common during intercourse with a partner. Despite the capacity and the desire to ejaculate, some clients report that they can eventually ejaculate with a partner but only after lengthy and vigorous stimulation. Some describe giving up after a prolonged effort as a result of discomfort on their own part or on the part of their partner. While episodic ejaculation difficulties are not uncommon as men age, men with DE often report ejaculation having been a problem at all ages.

Many men with DE have no difficulty with erections or ejaculating in a reasonable time while masturbating, especially when alone. Some have no difficulty ejaculating in the presence of their partners while masturbating or with manual or oral stimulation by their partner, but cannot do so during vaginal or anal intercourse.

For some couples, delayed or absent ejaculation is not an issue. It does not meet diagnostic criteria until the couple desires to become pregnant. At this point it represents a diagnosable problem for one or both partners. For other couples, each partner may experience him- or herself as inadequate and the sexual encounter as unfulfilling as a result of the ejaculatory problem. Sometimes partners of men with DE attribute the problem to themselves because of feeling unattractive, rejected, or unlovable.

Etiology and Assessment

There are multiple factors that contribute to the onset and continuation of DE. A variety of medical, psychological, relationship, and cultural contributors to the problem must be fully assessed.

Medical factors contributing to DE include: hormonal deficits, especially having to do with androgen levels; diabetic neuropathy; prostate cancer treatment; the ingestion of 5-alpha reductase inhibitors for enlarged prostate or hair loss; any illness or surgery that interferes with the pelvic nervous system; penile desensitization particularly with aging; and anti-depressants such as SSRIs. Perelman and Rowland (2006) suggest that the primary cause of DE may be a combination of the individual man's neurological predisposition, producing a range of ejaculatory latency across men, and of a variety of factors operating in any particular encounter, producing a range of ejaculatory latency for each individual man in different situations. Some men with DE report a history of *bladder shyness.* Anxiety may contribute to other biomedical-related etiologies.

On the psychological level, any emotional state that inhibits the orgasmic reflex can affect ejaculation. This includes feelings of anxiety and attentional distraction, both of which can shift the man's focus away from the very stimulation on which he needs to focus to be orgasmic. Kaplan and early psychodynamic theorists also suggested that internal psychological conflict might be associated with DE. The intrapsychic strife may be connected to a fear of pregnancy, relationship involvement, hostility towards the partner, resistance to pleasure, fears of castration, and even sadistic impulses towards partners, among others. Other theorists have suggested that the anxieties and attentional distractions are associated with poor communication about the desired type of stimulation and other sexual needs (Masters & Johnson, 1970; Perelman, 2014). This is one reason it is so important to ask during the assessment about whether the man tells his partner in detail about the way he prefers to be stimulated.

Other psychological factors that affect ejaculation include worries about body image (Perelman & Rowland, 2006) and a preference for sex by themselves (Apfelbaum, 2000).

Modifications for Diverse Populations

Perelman has reviewed the literature and identifies three factors that are strongly associated with DE: a high rate of masturbation (three or more times per week); a distinctive masturbatory pattern that is difficult for a partner to replicate (such as using extreme thigh pressure); and "a disparity between the reality of sex with a partner compared with preferred sexual fantasies during masturbation" (Perelman, 2014, p. 141).

As a result, some clinicians suspect that the growing use of online pornography may affect delayed or absent ejaculation with a partner. However, this is currently a controversial theory.

When it comes to relationship issues, resentment and hostility that have built up within the context of the couple's sexual and non-sexual interactions require consideration. This is particularly true when there is pressure to, or fears of, conceiving (Althof, Rubio-Aurioles, & Perelman, 2012). It is not uncommon for more introverted or reserved men who are apprehensive about expressing their feelings to displace their resentments onto their sexual interactions, unconsciously or subconsciously conditioning themselves to withhold ejaculation.

Family beliefs about sex, and cultural and religious conservatism, can also influence the development of DE (Masters & Johnson, 1970). Any environment that reinforces a negative perception of sexual expression, and especially ejaculation, increases the likelihood of delayed orgasm.

Specific Treatment Modifications of Sensate Focus for Delayed Ejaculation
As there is currently no medical procedure that aids the treatment of DE, therapy moves immediately to Sensate Focus.

Individual Sessions
Much like the treatment of pain and penetration disorders, the treatment of DE may begin with the client spending individual time prior to initiating couple's Sensate Focus, time devoted to everything but self-stimulating to orgasm. He is asked to stop his regular self-stimulation habits and encouraged not to orgasm until he is able to ejaculate with his partner. Sensate Focus self-exploration is suggested with three goals including helping him identify the specific touch and fantasy stimuli: he finds most arousing; that parallel what he would like to find stimulating with his partner; and that he already does find stimulating with his partner. The man experiencing DE identifies the type of stimulation he requires to ejaculate with a partner in terms of degree of pressure, speed, or location of touch. The characteristic that is most common among men who confront DE is lack of adequately arousing stimulation. This is often the case because men tend to stimulate themselves more vigorously and with greater pressure whereas their partners, especially female partners, may stimulate them less intensely and with lighter pressure using their own frame of reference for preferred stimulation pressure.

During these self-Sensate Focus opportunities, the DE client initially spends time focusing on touch sensations that are most absorbing, with the understanding that ejaculation is not the goal. He is directed to stop short of orgasm as this not only removes the demand pressure for ejaculating but also begins retraining his self-stimulation triggers to approximate those he would like to experience with his partner. If his grip has been significantly firmer than the sensations of vaginal or anal stimulation can possibly replicate, he is asked to use a lighter touch.

Couple Sessions

The next step is to desensitize the ejaculatory response to partner interaction in a step-wise fashion by having the couple initiate touching with breasts, chest, and genitals off limits, and then moving them on through the Sensate Focus hierarchy. During this involvement with the partner, the man learns to stimulate himself and ejaculate in his partner's presence. The next successive approximation is to have him learn to ejaculate with his partner providing part or all of the skin-to-skin contact. Then the couple cooperates with insertion just as ejaculatory inevitability (the first stage of male orgasm) approaches.

Stimulation and Code Word

All this time, the client communicates to his partner the type of stimulation he finds most effective, non-verbally if possible but also verbally if necessary. The partner is asked to stimulate vigorously and, if the client experiences himself being distracted by old, inhibitory thoughts, he uses a previously agreed-upon code word, much as do the clients with ED, to suggest a change in position and/or the type of stimulation he receives from his partner.

Fantasy and Other Helpful Techniques

Unlike other clients with sexual dysfunctions, men with DE are encouraged to focus on whatever sensory stimulation they find absorbing and arousing, including not just touch sensations but also visual sensations, fantasy, verbal communication, bodily movement, and anything else that will facilitate their becoming mindfully absorbed in the experience with their partners.

Much as with FOD, the importance of varied stimulation from a number of sources with elements of surprise cannot be overemphasized. For example, stopping and starting intercourse rather than staying the course once insertion begins may provide the extra stimulation needed.

Additional therapeutic adjustments may include PC exercises to tone and provide release of overly tense PC muscles, and deep breathing techniques to help stimulate calming, parasympathetic responses.

Genital Pelvic Pain Disorder (Dyspareunia) and Penetration Disorder (Vaginismus)
Definition

Genital Pelvic Pain Disorder and Penetration Disorder include pain of various intensities occurring in different locations in the genital pelvic area. This pain occurs most often when there are attempts to touch the painful area but it can even occur when touch is merely anticipated. Included in this diagnosis are Vulvodynia, a burning pain for which there are no apparent or obvious physical findings, and Vaginismus, the reflexive spasms in the outer third of the vaginal barrel that are an intensification of normal, voluntary muscles guarding the vaginal opening in anticipation of pain, fear, or anxiety, or manifesting as a phobic response. Despite the fact that the *DSM-5* and other definitional schemes emphasize pain with insertion, we are also going to include difficulty and pain not necessarily associated specifically with insertion or thoughts about insertion. With this in mind, common characteristics include:

Modifications for Diverse Populations

1. Difficulty and pain with insertion or touch to the affected area;
2. Anxiety just thinking about the potential of pain with insertion or touch to the affected area; and/or
3. The defensive reflex of a spasmodic tightening of the pelvic floor muscles during attempts at insertion, touch to the affected area, or thoughts of touch to the affected area.

Prevalence

Genital Pelvic Pain Disorder (Dyspareunia) is present in approximately 15% of women in North America. Penetration Disorder (Vaginismus) prevails in somewhere between 0.4 and 6.0%. The rates are higher in areas of the world where there is a lack of adequate sex education and much sexual inhibition. Vaginismus is often undiagnosed or misdiagnosed by medical professionals and therapists alike, especially in its mild to moderate forms.

There is little information on its occurrence in transgender populations or related to anal pain in Gay populations. However, recent research includes the possibility that men may also experience Genital Pain and Dyspareunia (Bergeron, Rosen, & Pukall, 2014).

Presentation

Genital Pelvic Pain Disorder and the pain associated with Penetration Disorder are often described as burning, cutting, shooting, or throbbing. The pain may be felt around the entire vulva, just at one spot, at the vaginal opening, or deeper within the vagina. It may be present throughout insertion or just at the beginning, during urination, during a gynecologic exam, or when the client is attempting to use tampons.

Sometimes the Dyspareunic or Vaginismic client experiences pain at the beginning of insertion and it diminishes as she continues with intercourse. Other women experience so much distress that insertion is impossible and must be stopped. Sometimes the pain continues for a time even after attempts at intercourse have ended.

There is also variability in the type of sexual interest and responsiveness reported by those with Genital Pelvic Pain or Penetration Disorders. Some report experiencing a satisfactory sex life, especially with Vaginismus, and come for therapy only when they want to conceive and are unable to do so. Others report experiencing an almost phobic response to any attempts at, or thoughts about attempts related to, sexual activity of any type.

Both partners may come for therapy without being aware of the specific Dyspareunic or Vaginismic nature of the sexual dysfunction. Instead, they may present as a case of lack of desire, disorder, *unconsummated* sexual relationship, and even ED (later determined as having developed secondarily as a reaction to the pained partner's distress).

Etiology and Assessment

Dyspareunia and Vaginismus may be a result of biomedical problems and these usually need to be ruled out first. In addition to the effects of aging (decreasing lubrication, thinning of the vaginal walls), surgery, and treatments for infertility, chronic illnesses, and cancer, biomedical factors may include

Early puberty and pain with first tampon use, vulvovaginal and urinary tract infections, early and prolonged use of oral contraceptives, nociceptor proliferation and sensitization, and lower touch and pain thresholds ... Recurrent yeast infections can cause persistent vulvar pain ... Abnormalities of the [pelvic floor muscle] while at rest, including hypertonicity and poor muscles control, hypersensitivity, and increased mucosal sensitivity, may close the vaginal hiatus and thus interfere with penetration. Women may also exhibit a defensive reaction of the PFM [pelvic floor muscle] during attempted vaginal penetration. A vicious cycle involving the pain and further muscle dysfunction makes it difficult to identify cause and effect and is complicated by the involvement of psychosocial factors.

(Bergeron, Rosen, & Pukall, 2014, p. 161)

Other etiological factors may include environmental sensitivities and allergies. Particularly in the case of Vaginismus, pain experienced during the first attempt or attempts at insertion, pelvic exams, and infertility treatment can contribute significantly to the onset of the disorder.

Other individual and psychological factors include a history of physical or emotional abuse, and sexual trauma that may increase the likelihood of genital and pelvic distress as much as four- to six-fold. In general, low self-esteem and developmental immaturity are reported as positively correlated with pain or penetration dysfunctions. Anxious or somatizing personality styles or disorders, where there is a tendency to catastrophize about physical distress and pain, are often associated with a greater likelihood of suffering Genital Pelvic Pain or Penetration Disorder. This is also true of those who fear losing control in response to pain, or who channel anxiety into physical distress.

There are a number of interpersonal factors that may contribute to Genital Pain and Penetration Disorders. These include poor sexual technique, partner pressure, and lack of partner support. The Dyspareunic person who feels compelled to engage in sexual activity in order to avoid negative consequences in the relationship, or who believes they are not psychologically or physically ready for sexual activity, has a higher likelihood of developing pain-related dysfunctions.

As with most other dysfunctions, situational stressors that include overwhelming family and work responsibilities contribute to the increased likelihood of experiencing Dyspareunia or Vaginismus. Cultural factors, like belief in the painful loss of virginity, are also associated with the development of these disorders. Vaginismus, in particular, is more common in sexually conservative cultures.

Specific Treatment Modifications of Sensate Focus for Genital Pelvic Pain (Dyspareunia)
and Penetration Disorder (Vaginismus)
The most important part of any sexual pain treatment is that the client must experience herself as being in total control of the experience. This begins with a detailed medical exam by a well-trained gynecologist or pelvic floor specialist, conducted to confirm the diagnosis and identify biomedical problems. The person conducting the examination prepares the client carefully, reassuring her that there will not be any vaginal penetration, that she can ask for a pause or to stop at any time, that she will be engaged throughout, and that she is encouraged to provide feedback during the exam.

Psychosocial factors contributing to the disorder may also have to be addressed. These include clinically significant problems including a history of trauma, affective disorders, severe couple's conflict, and the partner's individual and/or sexual issues.

Modifications for Diverse Populations

Medical Treatments

Some clients may choose an exclusively medical treatment approach such as the use of topical applications, oral or vaginally administered anti-anxiety medications, Botox, or surgery. Clients may also elect pelvic floor specialists and biofeedback training. Neither of these approaches precludes the use of a coordinated intervention that also includes sex and relationship therapy.

The Sex Therapy Approach: Education, Individual Sessions, Fingers, and Dilators

Most sex therapy with Genital Pelvic Pain/Penetration Disorders begins with sexuality education emphasizing the role of the pelvic floor muscles in the pain disorder, and the role of the fear–avoidance loop. In the case of Vaginismus, mindfulness training coupled with the use of the woman's own fingers or a set of graduated dilators in a systematically desensitizing fashion is usually suggested. The client may use the dilators by herself in combination with pelvic floor training, and also with increased awareness of her PC muscles.

When it comes to Sensate Focus proper, treatment usually begins with the Dyspareunic or Vaginismic client's initially engaging in *daily* touching sessions by herself, focusing on tactile sensations as usual. This might be likened to pairing systematic desensitization treatment with *in vivo* exposure therapy during which the client is encouraged to confront and manage her fears, and become desensitized to them as she slowly moves up a hierarchy of increasingly anxiety-provoking experiences. These sessions are paired with mindfulness training to manage the anxiety in which the client practices returning her attention to the tactile sensations as well as to her breathing. This sometimes takes place in the bath and may be followed by genital self-discovery. Before any attempts at inserting a finger or dilator, the client may be encouraged to let go of her anxious tension using PC practice, orgasmic release, deep breathing, and/or guided imagery.

Next, she practices insertion with her fingers and/or vaginal dilators in order to further desensitize her anxieties around contact and insertion. This begins with the smallest finger or dilator or, if these are too large, with just the tip of a Q-tip. It is lightly placed near her vaginal opening or close to the perineum. It is suggested she contract, or tighten, her PC muscles as much as she can, counting silently to herself, "One thousand one, one thousand two, one thousand three" and then letting go of the pelvic tension. She does this three times in a row, then takes a 10-second break, then does another set of three 3-second contractions, takes another break, and then does a third and final set. She practices these sets of three 3-second contractions three times, for a total of nine PC muscle-tightening/releasing repetitions.

The client practices these sets of three 3-second contractions as long as she needs to in order to feel comfortable, or at least less uncomfortable, with having her finger or the dilator in this position. A good indicator of when the client is ready to progress is when she comes into therapy reporting feeling bored or uninterested in the sessions rather than anxious.

The next step is to repeat this sequence of three 3-second contractions as the woman moves in small increments closer to inserting either her little finger or the smallest dilator into her vagina. She then attempts another group of three sets of three 3-second contractions. Slowly and in a step-wise fashion, she moves closer to inserting the finger or dilator with each group of contractions, and is strongly encouraged when removing her finger or the dilator to take as many steps as she took inserting. Sensing her new control, she is less likely to set off any unwelcome and painful contractions.

When the client has managed her avoidance and moderated her anxiety, she is encouraged to move on to the next larger dilator. She will have greater confidence in her ability to experience insertion without pain when she has traced the circumference size of her partner's *glans* or partner's dildo and knows that she has been able to comfortably insert a dilator matching this circumference size.

It bears repeating that the client is always in complete control in terms of placement, depth, and moving on with the next largest finger or dilator, all in supportive collaboration with her treating professional. The client is encouraged to practice all of these skills at least once if not twice a day for six out of seven days a week and for as many weeks as it takes until she reports feeling less fearful and is catastrophizing less often about insertion. The time frame required for working in individual sessions can vary tremendously from client to client.

Couple Sessions

Partnered Sensate Focus suggestions are given shortly after the Vaginismic client begins feeling less uncomfortable with the self-insertion process and is ready to engage in a couple's experience. Suggestions often then follow the usual hierarchical steps and lead to the non-demand, sensory-oriented atmosphere that may further help the client let go of her tension. However, the woman may, after practicing by herself for a period of time, decide to include her partner in her own touching sessions prior to beginning the couples portion of Sensate Focus. This can be left up to her.

When formal couple's Sensate Focus begins, after genitals are on limits in the touching, and perhaps after she has been orgasmic, the woman inserts either her finger, her partner's finger or, more likely by this time, the smallest graduated dilator. Then she slowly alternates tensing and letting go of her PC muscles around it, and holds it inside for a time. Later the client can practice slowly moving the dilator while in the presence of the partner. The partner can be involved in holding, touching, and being supportively present. As her comfort level increases, the client can use larger fingers and/or increasingly larger dilators.

Some women prefer not to use their fingers or a dilator in the partner's presence and to proceed to female astride. They can then play outside the vaginal opening, tensing and releasing the PC muscles while being touched by the partner until they feel ready to move back onto the penis and slowly insert using the skills practiced with the dilator or their largest fingers. Her next step is experimenting slowly with movement and depth, again, staying focused on temperature, pressure, and texture, and changing her action if she experiences any discomfort.

Before doing any inserting, the woman is encouraged to practice the skills she has mastered in the individual finger or dilator sessions. She tightens her PC muscles three times in sets of three 3-second contractions. Then she lets go of the contractions, inserts fingers, the dilator, or her partner's penis a little further to whatever degree she would like, and then continues the process. If pain occurs, she is encouraged *not* to grin and bear it. Instead, she breathes, contracts her PC muscles even more tightly and paradoxically than they are already, and removes the penis, finger, or dilator systematically, in a step-wise fashion, so as to avoid triggering any defensive contractions.

Modifications for Diverse Populations

Having said all of this in terms of the procedures, variations are sometimes helpful. For example, couple's Sensate Focus during which the woman is orgasmic might actually precede and then be followed by the woman's exploring by herself or in the company of her partner with finger or dilator insertion. This is because her arousal and orgasmic response may help her feel connected to her partner, less anxious, and less physiologically tense.

As an addition to the systematic desensitization provided by the use of finger, dilator, or penile insertion during Sensate Focus, treatment of Genital Pain and Penetration Disorders is even more effective when coupled with anxiety management and cognitive-behavior therapy skills that address catastrophizing, pain hypervigilance, and negative self-judging affective and thought patterns, among others.

LGBTQ, Sex and Gender Variant, Kink, and Non-Monogamous Clients

For the most part, Masters and Johnson developed their model for Sensate Focus with heterosexual couples. Although the original research on male and female sexual response published in *Human Sexual Response* (1966) was carried out with identified Gay, Lesbian and heterosexual individuals and couples, a complex and sophisticated understanding of sexual orientation and gender fluidity had barely been articulated at that time.

Over the past four decades, since the publication of Masters and Johnson's original Sensate Focus protocol, most clinicians have recognized the vastness of, and variation in, human sexual expression. Hall and Graham (2014), Iasenza (2010), Leiblum and Rosen (2007), and Nichols (1982) have offered excellent reflections and research findings on these subjects. These clinicians and investigators have moved from a model of sexual *deviance* to one of sexual *variation*. In general, "members of sexual minorities now seek sex therapy not for help in changing or accepting their orientation but for help improving their sexual satisfaction" (Nichols, 2014). The old, rigid categories for labeling individuals in terms of sexual orientation, gender identification, and non-mainstream sexual interests have begun to fall away.

The initialism *LGBTQ* refers to Lesbian, Gay, Bisexual, Transgender, and Queer and/or Questioning. It acknowledges that many individuals do not fit comfortably into neat sexual categories. It is associated with other descriptions such as *sex and gender fluid*, *sex and gender variant*, *kinky*, and *gender nonconforming*, among others, in an effort to capture the non-binary, intersecting, and versatile nature of gender identification, sexual orientation, and expression. Research suggests that these groups of clients, particularly bisexual women, are more likely to express sexual interests that are not considered mainstream. These may include:

1. Bondage and discipline, dominance/submission, and sadomasochism (BDSM);
2. Unconventional sexual practices, concepts, identities, and fantasies;
3. Alternative relationships (multiple sexual and romantic partners, or *polyamory*); and
4. Open relationships (sometimes referred to as *ethical non-monogamy*).
    (Barker & Langdridge, 2010; Richters, de Visser, Rissel, Grulich, & Smith, 2008)

Even so-called conventional sexual interests are more fluid than has been previously appreciated. We have witnessed the sometimes inclusion of BDSM play into what are considered mainstream practices since the publication of the best seller, *Fifty Shades of Grey* (James, 2011). Not surprisingly, research findings on the sex lives and sexual difficulties of minority and non-traditional individuals and couples are even more limited than the results on hetero-sexuals with conventional sexual interests. With these qualifications in mind we will proceed to describe the most common sexual difficulties of Lesbian and Gay couples, and make suggestions for modifications in Sensate Focus that may be helpful. We will follow with a few comments on work with transgender clients and other sexual minorities.

Lesbian Sexuality

Depending on which findings you consider, somewhere between 2 and 8% of women identify as Lesbians and/or Bisexual. Bailey and his colleagues (2016) suggest that the prevalence is probably less than 5%. Even though this is less than what the average American guestimates (as high as 25%), it is still a sizable portion of the population and clinicians are increasingly receiving requests from Lesbian couples for sex therapy.

Presentation

The most common sexual complaint of Lesbian women is their own or their partner's lack of sexual desire despite the absence of major conflicts, and in the presence of both good communication and physical affection. The initiation of sex seems to be particularly susceptible. Some of the first researchers to explore Lesbian sexual patterns suggest that Lesbians have less frequent sexual encounters than other partnerships (Blumstein & Schwartz, 1983). The term "Lesbian death bed" has been coined to describe the loss of sexual frequency in these long-term relationships. Women in Lesbian relationships may differ from heterosexual women in that their sexual interest may more often follow rather than precede sexual interaction (Basson, 2000).

Nevertheless, other researchers have discovered that while sexual encounters between Lesbians may be less frequent and less genitally focused, they include more sensuality and last for longer periods of time (Iasenza, 2002). Still others have identified Lesbians as being: more frequently orgasmic in their sexual encounters; less likely to have sex just for their partner's sake when they themselves are disinterested; less likely to report pain disorders; and less likely to have sexually transmitted infections (Nichols, 2014). Lesbian sexual relationships also appear to be characterized by the enduring eroticism of butch/femme identities, the exploration of gender dynamics, and their egalitarian nature (Lev & Nichols, 2015). This egalitarianism, together with the associated intense emotional and sexual connection between the partners, may result in a sense of symbiosis. The mystery that can add an extra and elemental spark of eroticism to their sexual relationship may be absent (Nichols, 2014).

Specific Treatment Modifications of Sensate Focus for Lesbian couples

Experts who work with Lesbian couples report that, for the most part, they do not significantly alter Sensate Focus procedures or instructions when working with Lesbian couples. In a personal communication (March 31, 2016), Suzanne Iasenza, a specialist working with Lesbian and Queer clients, suggests, "Because the goal is the development of presence instead of the achievement of a particular physical act ('being' vs. 'doing')" there is no need to change the Sensate Focus activities when working with Lesbian as opposed to heterosexual couples.

Modifications for Diverse Populations

Low Desire

The treatment of low desire in Lesbian women is similar to its treatment in heterosexual women. In an effort not to repeat information that has already been presented, please refer above to the section on *Female Sexual Interest/Arousal Disorder* (p. 68).

Genital-to-Genital Contact

As with all couples, the Lesbian couple's goals and preferred sexual practices are to be considered when suggesting a hierarchy of touch suggestions. In creating the Sensate Focus hierarchy, the only routine change that usually needs to be made has to do with the genital-to-genital contact. The couple may decide what position they would like to assume in this step. Is one of the partners going to be on top rubbing her *mons* area on the *mons* area of the other partner? Or would assuming a side-by-side scissoring position be preferable?

Insertion

The next issue to be considered is insertive sexual contact. Do they practice insertion of any kind? If not, would they like to? If so, would they prefer insertion using their fingers? Would they rather use a strap-on or a dildo? When Sensate Focus moves from resolving a sexual dysfunction (Sensate Focus 1) to enhancing the relationship (Sensate Focus 2), is oral sex something they would like to experience or with which they have difficulty?

Gay Male Sexuality

As with women and the Lesbian population, Gay men are thought to make up somewhere between 2 and 8% of men, most likely right around 5% (Bailey et al., 2016). Gay couples are similarly interested in resolving sexual dysfunctions and cultivating sexual optimization, and are increasingly knocking on the door of sex therapists.

Presentation

Gay male couples, like Lesbian couples, are more similar to all other couples than they are different. However, they do seem to report a lower rate both of Premature and Delayed Ejaculation as well as fewer concerns with out-of-control or problematic sexual behavior. This is despite the fact that research findings also suggest Gay men experience a higher overall rate of sexual dysfunction in general, and ED in particular (Bancroft, Carnes, Janssen, Goodrich, & Long, 2005; Sandfort & de Keizer, 2001). They also report a higher number of consensual non-monogamous relationships and a higher overall number of casual sex partners and sexual frequency than heterosexual men or women.

While Gay couples practice anal sex less often than oral sex or mutual masturbation, and while Gay couples who do practice it do not necessarily include it in every sexual encounter, when they do report sexual difficulties associated with anal sex it often has to do with disagreements over the role of *insertee* (top) vs. that of the *inserter* (bottom). Another difficulty therapists may encounter is aversion to anal sex or painful anal sex, sometimes associated with sexual trauma. One increasing concern among this population is the rising rate of HIV transmission (Center for Disease Control and Prevention, 2015). This has led to *harm reduction* techniques, including *serosorting*. Serosorting involves identifying the status of possible partners before engaging in unprotected anal sex and using PrEP, a controversial antiretroviral drug, in small doses while HIV negative.

Specific Treatment Modifications of Sensate Focus for Gay Couples

Much as with Lesbian couples, sex therapist Joe Kort suggests that he does not significantly alter Sensate Focus procedures or suggestions when working with Gay as opposed to heterosexual couples (personal communication, March 31, 2011). Sex therapy for Gay couples is individualized and directed towards their goals as well as incorporating their sexual preferences. One of the Sensate Focus modifications includes the choice of positions for the genital-to-genital contact. These may include kneeling on the bed while facing one another, or lying face-to-face, or some other position.

Another modification with Gay couples has to do with the treatment of ED. In using Sensate Focus with heterosexual ED couples, the female client goes astride her partner, directs the genital-to-genital contact, and does the inserting when she is ready and when she knows there is sufficient engorgement for her partner to be ready. As a result, the client with ED does not have to be concerned about the insertion. For Gay couples who practice anal sex, this is obviously not the case. It can be somewhat more difficult to replicate this non-spectatoring approach if the ED client is the *top* or inserter. In these instances, including additional practical suggestions for gaining and losing engorgement may be helpful for managing fears of performance. Sensate Focus modifications for Gay couples may emphasize directing attention to visual sensations. These alterations may include an emphasis on visual sensations especially when spectatoring their own arousal.

In cases of rapid ejaculation, one important modification is the position for touching with chest and genitals on limits. It is important for the person being touched, even if he feels somewhat vulnerable, to stay in the position where he is lying down on his back, facing towards the ceiling, and lying in between his partner's outspread legs rather than sitting up in front of his partner to allow application of the Coronal Squeeze.

Bisexuality, Pansexuality, and Other Orientations and Identities

In recent years there has been more acceptance of bisexuality, pansexuality, and asexuality among others as valid sexual orientations, especially among younger age groups. Studies seem to point to the likelihood that bisexuality is more common among women than men, with three times more women identifying as bisexual as opposed to Lesbian (Gartrell, Bos, & Goldberg, 2012). These figures may be somewhat skewed because they rely on self-identification rather than sexual behavior or fantasy. They also may not include the category of heterosexually identified men who have sex with men (MSM) but who may not consider themselves bisexual.

Presentation

According to sex therapist Margaret Nichols, Ph.D., "many self identified bisexuals are also transgender, 'kinky,' or polyamorous" (2014, p. 325). This requires the clinician to be informed, comfortable with, and sensitive to these diversities, or be prepared to refer clients to clinicians who are. One of the more common concerns in couples in which one partner is identified as bi- or pansexual is the fear that the partner will decide to become involved with a partner of the *alternative* gender. This raises the ongoing concern that this partner will decide he or she is more heterosexual or Lesbian or Gay than originally suspected and the fit between the couple may evaporate.

Specific Treatment Modifications of Sensate Focus for Bi- and Pansexual Couples
Bisexual and pansexual partners, regardless of gender or other identifications, have not been sufficiently studied to determine what, if any, sexual dysfunctions or difficulties they experience that are different from heterosexuals, Lesbian, or Gay identified clients. There do not appear to be any significant changes in Sensate Focus suggestions for this population unless gleaned from the client history-taking sessions and in consideration of the clients' goals.

Transgender or Gender Queer Couples
Transgender people can be a rewarding population with which to work in sex therapy. They represent the most recent chorus of minority groups seeking inclusion, legal protection, social justice, and access to health and mental health care.

Presentation
The research on transgender and gender queer individuals is exceedingly limited (Colebunders, De Cuypere, & Monstrey, 2015). What we do know, however, is that gender refers to one's personal sense of *maleness*, *femaleness*, or *gender fluidity/variance*. This personal sense is related in complex fashion to self-concept and is not simply compliance to gender roles (how one is expected to live out his/her gender identity) or sexual orientation (the type or person to whom one is currently sexually attracted, if any). There is an increasing acceptance of the fact that there is much variation in gender identities beyond the conventional male/female dichotomy. In fact, the author of a recent publication encourages professionals to educate their trans clients that accepting their trans identities and bodies as they are without using hormones or surgical intervention may also be a valid way for them to proceed (Sieber, 2012).

Within the population of transgender-identified people, a subset has recently been identified as persons who may also be diagnosed on the Autism Spectrum. The most non-binary gender-identified individuals may be people who are on the Spectrum and who also identify as trans (Kristensen & Broome, 2015).

Specific Treatment Modifications of Sensate Focus for Transgender Clients
Trans-identified individuals who are seeking gatekeeping services for genital alignment surgery consult many sex therapists. However, since the subject of this manual is the use of Sensate Focus, we are not going to go into detail about medical transitioning. Instead, we are going to focus on working with clients who are already transitioning or have completed transition. We are going to discuss the adaptations of Sensate Focus that are helpful for these couples. Information on the guidelines for professionals working with transition can be obtained by visiting the website of the World Professional Association for Transgender Health at www.wpath.org.

In the last three decades, the age at which many trans-identified individuals come forward with gender-related concerns has dropped considerably. The significance of this is that fewer grow to adulthood without making their transitions, and fewer marry and have children, only later to identify as transgender. This has reduced the number of heartbreaking scenarios that used to play out in our offices whereby life partners had to grapple with whether or not to stay together in modified relationships or change their own sexual orientation.

Much like therapy with cisgender couples, sex therapist Suzanne Iasenza (2010) describes the use of Sensate Focus with transgender clients as primarily cultivating a state of mindfulness. She does not modify Sensate Focus significantly when working with this population.

Male-to-Female Trans Clients

Despite treating fewer couples that must wrestle with these difficult decisions, male-to-female trans individuals on hormones still present with sexual difficulties in their relationships. This is usually associated with desire difficulties. While the trans client may experience changes in desire as an extremely meaningful and even enjoyable female *rite of passage* as well as a relief from the *tyranny of testosterone* and ego dystonic erections, their partners may not be so enthusiastic. Sometimes partners process the loss of sexual interest and capacity as disturbing if only because the change is not of their own choosing.

In situations where both partners desire an increase in sexual interest and sexually connected involvement, Sensate Focus can be a useful medium to reduce goal-oriented attitudes, increase sensual interaction, fuel sexual thoughts and feelings, and aid the discovery of sexual relating and release with which they are more psychologically comfortable. Just as with addressing interest and arousal in non-trans women, self-Sensate Focus, fantasy development and other enrichment techniques can be useful.

The structure of the Sensate Focus hierarchy depends on the trans client's view of her body. While some pre-op male-to-female trans people are comfortable with genital stimulation, erections, and insertion, others are not. Some prefer to have their genitals secured and covered at all times; others are at ease with rubbing *mons* areas together for stimulation rather than being touched directly. The critical issue here is that the therapist must work in a collaborative fashion with the trans client and her partner to determine what is most helpful for that particular couple. Additionally, the therapist needs to encourage the partners to negotiate how the non-trans partner will provide and be provided release as desired.

Female-to-Male Trans Clients

The number of people transitioning from female-to-male has recently equaled that of the previously more common male-to-female trans individuals (Beemyn & Rankin, 2011). Two-thirds of these individuals first identified as *butch* Lesbians. A number of investigations suggest that these *transmen* are blending sexual orientation and gender identity into more varied and non-binary identities. Those under 40 are identifying themselves more as *gender queer.* They report having a more fluid sense of their gender, sexual attraction, and orientation. They also are less conventional in their transitioning expectations and desires: they are not automatically heading towards hormone replacement or genital surgery.

The most common sexual difficulties presented by female-to-male trans clients, besides the ones that come to light during the self-discovery and transitioning process itself, can be the trans client's higher sexual drive and interest, often a byproduct of testosterone treatment. Previously well-matched couples, especially couples that are now transmen and their cisgendered female partners, may find themselves at odds over sexual frequency. This may result in loss of sexual desire by the cisgendered female partners. As a result, these couples are best treated by using Sensate Focus in a way that mirrors its use with clients troubled by FSIAD. The same can be said if the cisgendered partner is male. In this situation Sensate Focus would be used in a way that reflects partners' experiencing Male HSDD.

Kink

Kink is considered engagement in unconventional or non-traditional sexual activities, concepts, fantasies, or scenarios in order to increase sexual arousal and intimacy between partners. In contrast to *vanilla* or *straight* sexual behavior, Kink derives from the sense of change in direction, or *bend*, in sexual behavior and preferences.

People of all sexual orientations and walks of life practice kinky or unconventional sex. They may participate once in a lifetime or make it a lifestyle. They may even be unaware of the moniker and yet practice it in the privacy of their bedrooms, or they may be fully identified with the lifestyle in the public arena. One study suggests that heterosexual men and women are the least likely to practice Kink activities as defined by bondage and discipline, dominance and submission, and sadomasochism (BDSM), and bisexual men and particularly women are most likely. Nonetheless, somewhere between 12 and 55% of these populations have either restrained someone or been restrained for sexual arousal. Between 4 and 36% have received or inflicted pain for pleasure (Breyer, Smith, Eisenberg, Ando, Rowen, & Shindel, 2010).

Presentation

Kink may include *fetishism*, *BDSM*, sexual objectification, and a host of very specific sexual interests currently categorized as *Paraphilic Disorders* in the *DSM-5*. In recent years people in the Kink community have begun to question the appropriateness of including these categorizations as diagnostic criteria in the *DSM-5* since, just as Gay and Lesbian people used to be included in this classification system, they may represent a normal variation in sexual interest and not as a diagnosable abnormality, especially under circumstances of consent.

Specific Treatment Modifications of Sensate Focus for Kink Clients

In a personal communication (March 29, 2016), Margaret Nichols, Ph.D., who specializes in work with the Kink community, suggests that there is no need to modify the specific Sensate Focus procedures and suggestions when working with kinky clients. Neil Cannon, Ph.D., LMFT, another sex therapist familiar with the Kink community, concurs. He advises that the changes in Sensate Focus with clients from the Kink community often have not so much to do with the actual process of the touching opportunities, that is, not so much with changes in the actual positions, pacing, or activities. For the most part, clinicians using Sensate Focus with Kink clients follow the standard protocol. Instead, most alterations have more to do with the applications of Sensate Focus. Sensate Focus may be used as a bridge to help these clients when they are at an impasse in their intimate relationships, or with common sexual dysfunctions. Sensate Focus can serve as a *confidence booster* that reassures the client. Sensate Focus can also be used to help Kink couples slow down their sexual activity.

What follows is an example of using Sensate Focus as a transitional bridge with a couple that presented for therapy and was engaging in BDSM practices including a female partner who was submissive and who also suffered from Dissociative Identity Disorder. All of the partner's personalities were adult except for one that was a nine-year-old girl. The clients were concerned because they believed that BDSM play with the "young" girl violated the definition of consent. The couple not only started to disengage from BDSM sex but also from non-BDSM, mainstream sex. With this couple, Sensate Focus was used to help them re-engage first in non-BDSM sex and then as a transition for helping them back to BDSM that no longer included playing with the nine-year-old female alter.

With another couple, BDSM activities had been labeled as problematic because they had come to dominate their sex life. They had stopped having non-BDSM sex altogether. The male partner subsequently developed erectile problems when the couple tried to engage in non-BDSM sex and was feeling increasingly vulnerable. Because the couple still wanted to savor non-BDSM sex, Sensate Focus was implemented to help the partner with ED manage the anxiety-provoking distractions associated with his erections in this context. The Sensate Focus protocol, attitudes, and skills were identical to those used to help non-Kink partners resolve erectile dysfunction. However, they served not only as a transitional tool but also as a significant confidence enhancer and a way of slowing the sexual activity down. This provided more opportunity for exploring the varied sensual connection they could experience with each other.

Consensual, Non-Monogamous Couples

Consensual non-monogamy is the open agreement between two people that they are not going to be sexually exclusive with one another. In an article entitled, *What Psychology Professionals Should Know About Polyamory* (based on a paper presented at the 8th Annual Diversity Conference in March 1999 in Albany, New York), one researcher states,

> While openly polyamorous relationships are relatively rare ... there are indications that private polyamorous arrangements within relationships are actually quite common. Blumstein and Schwartz ... noted that of 3,574 married couples in their sample, 15–28% had an understanding that allows non-monogamy under some circumstances. The percentages are higher among cohabitating couples (28%), lesbian couples (29%) and gay male couples (65%).
>
> (Weitzman, 1999, p. 312)

Presentation

Couples who adopt a consensually non-monogamous relationship vary by the degree to which: they disclose their other relationships to their partner; they disclose the details of their other relationships; the other relationships are bound by structure and guidelines; and the other relationships include emotional involvement. Non-monogamous relationship styles may present in six different ways. According to Adam and Sherry Fisher (2016), these include:

Swinging

Swinger couples agree to have sex together and on a somewhat regular basis with other people with the full knowledge and usually the presence of both partners. Swingers appear to experience the greatest enjoyment viewing their partners with others than of any other non-monogamous individuals;

Polyamory

People who choose, with the knowledge and consent of, and often formalized agreement with, their partners, to engage in sexual activity with others but usually without their partner present are considered *polyamorous.* They do not necessarily consider deep emotional investment or long-term commitment necessary conditions for having sexual relationships with these other people. There are four types of polyamorous relationships:

1. Vee: This involves one person's having a separate relationship with two different people but these two other people do not know each other and are not involved with each other;
2. Triads: In these relationships, all three individuals know each other and may be involved with each other relationally and sexually;
3. Quads: This is a more complex arrangement in which four people are involved but each of the partners only knows two of the other three partners. Quad polyamorous relationships usually move into a triad simply because only three of the four ever know each other; and
4. Network polycule: This is the most complex matrix of all and involves many networks of polyamorous people, some or all of who may know each other. Most of polyamorous relationships are of this type.

Monogamish

These partners are mostly monogamous but occasionally become involved with someone else without the partner being present. They tend to have the most anxious attachment styles and experience the least satisfaction with the non-monogamous arrangement;

Don't Ask, Don't Tell

Couples involved in these partnerships agree to engage in other relationships but on the condition that these involvements are not shared with one another;

Anarchy

Partners in these relationships agree that they may engage in other relationships without any pre-established rules or conditions for disclosure including whether the relationship will be strictly sexual or emotional or a combination;

Polygamy

A polygamous relationship is one in which one partner has more than one spouse. When it involves one man having more than one wife it is referred to as polygyny; when it involves one woman having more than one husband it is referred to as polyandry.

Specific Treatment Modifications of Sensate Focus for Consensual, Non-Monogamous Clients

As with Kink clients, sex therapist Dr. Neil Cannon suggests that when Sensate Focus is used with polyamorous couples it is not so much the procedures that are altered as it is the manner, timing, and purpose of its application. It can be used, once again, as a link to other sexual activity, to having the monogamous sexual interaction slow down and become more exploratory, or as a morale booster. We have also found in our practice that when Sensate Focus is used with polyamorous couples, it often must be paired with more extensive work on the general relationship and on intimacy and communication outside of the bedroom, than with some other types of sexually distressed couples. The most common relationship difficulty experienced by polyamorous clients in the research and in our practices is that one partner is often more fluid and flexible in his or her conception of sexually and emotionally committed relationships than the other. This can often cause significant conflict and tension within the overall relationship.

For example, a heterosexual couple recently came to therapy for loss of desire on the part of the female partner. She was ten years older than her husband and she had married in her 40s. Her husband, unbeknownst to her at the time of their wedding, became involved in the polyamorous lifestyle while he was single. As their marital relationship progressed, and the husband grew less satisfied with monogamous sex, he introduced the notion of polyamorous sexual activities to his wife. She was upset by this, threatened that her husband would leave her because of what she perceived to be her inability to satisfy him sexually. As a result, their own sexual relationship diminished in frequency and in her desire for it. Sensate Focus was used to suggest a more exploratory and sensorally enlivening experience for the couple's own intimate interaction. As they progressed both with Sensate Focus and also with increased trust, connection, and vulnerabilities, the female partner became more secure that her husband found her interesting and arousing sensually and sexually. She was more confident that their relationship was his primary interest and not at risk. She even became willing to negotiate with him about his polyamorous proclivities. Although she did not want to participate in the lifestyle, she was willing to grant him a "hall pass" once a month. This arrangement worked well for both of them.

In another instance, a married heterosexual couple contracted with a male play partner to engage in sexual activity with the wife. Both the wife and the husband consented, and the woman and her male play partner agreed on the sexual scenario. However, during the sexual play, the male play partner violated the wife's consent and continued on to have non-consensual intercourse that constituted a rape. As a result, she lost all interest in sex, including with her husband. Sensate Focus was utilized much as with any trauma survivor. It proved invaluable in helping her slowly and systematically regain a sense of control of the physical activity, to work her way back to having an interest in and the capacity to be sexual with her husband again.

Chapter 8: Common Problems and Their Management in Sensate Focus

Now we will move away from the changes to Sensate Focus that help clients with specific dysfunctions and with dysfunctions in specific types of relationship. We are going to take a look at common problems that surface when implementing Sensate Focus with couples from all types of populations. Some or all of these problems are to be expected to some degree at the beginning of Sensate Focus. However, if they persist beyond the initial sets of instructions, this may be indicative of the need for other types of interventions either before or during sex therapy and Sensate Focus.

While being aware of the common problems is important, understanding how to address them is perhaps even more so. In training and supervising other clinicians, it has been our experience that they frequently report finding Sensate Focus ineffective when encountering these problems. Our approach is that it is the very fact that Sensate Focus elicits these problems that suggests its value and importance. When these problems arise it is not the time to do away with Sensate Focus but to reframe the problems as precisely the reasons clients are in therapy and then to continue with sex therapy and Sensate Focus as a way to manage and ultimately resolve them.

Delaying the Touching Sessions

Despite the fact that clients are told that they do not need to have any particular emotion prior to doing the touching sessions, especially pleasant anticipation, one of the most common problems is delaying/avoiding the touching sessions until late at night or right before coming in for therapy. Delaying often takes two forms. With both types, resistance may be handled by encouraging couples to formally schedule the touching sessions. It may also respond to partners developing a plan as to how to deal with the resistance.

More specifically, in the first type of delay, one partner (often the one without the identified problem) may be looking forward to the touching but the other fails to initiate until the last minute and is clearly doing it without enthusiasm or without what the partner perceives as an expectation of positive results. This frequently results in disappointment on the part of the partner eagerly anticipating the sessions, and these couples often arrive at the therapy sessions frustrated or angry at each other. This common scenario is handled by reminding the clients that they are not expected to look forward to the touching sessions, and that whatever happens before and during them is a snapshot of the dynamics that have brought them to therapy in the first place. The primary dynamic may be, for example, that one partner pressures and the other resists, and then this partner complies in a service organization mode in order to minimize the overt or even covert conflict.

A review of methods to address the anxiety that might, in this case, be getting in the way of initiation, and how to utilize the partner to help manage this anxiety, is offered. For example, the hesitant client may say,

> I have thought about initiating the session for three days now without mentioning it. I think the best way to handle this is to tell you about my struggle and ask you to hold me for a few minutes before we begin.

The proactive partner is now hesitant to say something for fear of being perceived as pressuring or interfering with the other client's initiation. He or she is also growing frustrated and anxious that the touching may not happen. This partner is encouraged to say something like,

> I'm anxious about doing the touching before our next session but know you are to initiate and I don't want to pressure you. But it would be helpful to me to know what you are thinking about this and what, if anything, I might do to help.

This interchange involves relationship and communication skills that are self-responsible, non-blaming, authentic, and focused on the couple as a team rather than as competitors. Besides a focus on communication, problem-solving, and managing feelings that get in the way, the couple might be encouraged to formally schedule their touching sessions, always with the caveat that a renegotiation is possible.

In the second type of delaying, partners may collude in postponing the touching, often citing busy schedules and associated fatigue. They may have developed a pattern of protecting themselves and each other from the anxiety, the fear of rejection, and the anticipated failure associated with trying. A common barrier is the unspoken belief that, "If we don't try we cannot fail." Once again this is best addressed by identifying the pattern, normalizing the resistance and offering the couple tools to communicate, address the feelings, and move ahead.

Non-Compliance

Among the most common difficulties with Sensate Focus suggestions is clients' failure to do the touching exercises at all, or failure to do them as suggested. Sometimes the couple has avoided the Sensate Focus suggestions completely. Not infrequently this may represent pressuring dynamics from the partner who continues to push the envelope. Sometimes the couple has begun Sensate Focus but it devolves into their engaging in old patterns of sexual interaction and even intercourse instead of continuing with the touching sessions. It may seem as if the couple is denying the existence of the sexual problem by engaging in what therapists refer to as a *flight into health*. This is especially true when partners have gone without physical contact for a long time. Sometimes it is the very instruction that nothing has to happen that frees them momentarily from their fears of performance and allows them to function in this flight into health fashion. It may be helpful to reiterate that the goal is to have them function in a more secure way sexually *for a long time and not just for the moment*. The Sensate Focus skills may help them understand what they can do differently from this point forward, for the duration of their relationship, if they slip back into old patterns. It is as if the therapist is suggesting, "I don't promise you will never again fail to get and keep an erection, but you will know exactly what happened and what you might remember to do next time. It will not be such a mystery any longer."

Regardless of the reason, failure to do the touching or going beyond suggestions is processed in therapy by addressing the fear, confusion, guilt, anxiety, expectations, discomfort, pressure, and problematic relational dynamics associated with it. At no point are clients chastised for non-compliance, and their understandable difficulties are normalized. In fact, their non-compliance can be interpreted positively as helping the therapist clearly identify the roadblocks that get in the way of working on the sexual dysfunction, and provides the opportunity for offering therapeutic strategies for managing these roadblocks that may include, but are not limited to, the following:

1. Reviewing the purpose of Sensate Focus;
2. Clarifying expectations;
3. Formally scheduling touching time and setting reminders;
4. Scheduling touching daily at a certain time so both head to the bedroom at that time;
5. Changing who initiates and who touches first; and
6. Identifying, communicating, and managing the anxieties alone or with the partner's assistance.

It is often helpful to discuss the fact that couple's anticipation of the touching is often more anxiety provoking than the touching itself. Clients often confirm this subsequently and report feeling relieved, cared for, and more intimately connected to their partners once they have completed the touching sessions ("That wasn't so bad!"). This sense of emotional closeness and relief from pressure for any particular outcome helps to lessen their worries. Nonetheless, problems with non-compliance can re-emerge with each new Sensate Focus suggestion.

One of the most common therapist contributions to non-compliance is failure to explain the rationale for using Sensate Focus. This is where Masters and Johnson's data on the characteristics of sexually functional people may be valuable. As we have noted, Masters and Johnson discovered that there are three techniques these highly sexually functional people shared, and they are: focusing on sensations for one's interest; focusing on one's own experience rather than on the partner's; and returning the focus of attention to sensations if distracted by anything else. These strategies are the foundation of their therapy and the portal into natural sexual responsiveness. In offering Sensate Focus suggestions, clients are told that the purpose of the exercise is to practice these skills in order to build the foundation of the house they want constructed.

Another inadvertent therapeutic contribution to non-compliance is making the mistake of giving up too quickly when clients appear unwilling to follow through with Sensate Focus. It is helpful for clinicians to see non-compliance as a resistance, like any other resistance, that needs to be understood and addressed.

Dislike Touching: Boring, Constraining, and Non-Spontaneous
It is not uncommon for clients to report feeling bored with or limited by the touching exercises. They often yearn for spontaneity and freedom. Although couples come to sex therapists for direction, they may chafe at first at the highly structured approach.

When clients report boredom or lack of spontaneity they are sometimes still steeped in demand expectations for enjoying, being excited by, responding sexually to the touching exercises, and/or expressing disappointment that they must begin where they are. It may be helpful to remind them that if they could make sexual responsiveness occur on demand they would already have done so. Their discontent with the touching suggestions has to be balanced with the necessity of taking small steps. Again, it may be helpful to characterize Sensate Focus as the foundation of therapy that must be built before the walls and roof of other techniques can be included.

At times it is the therapist who needs to be creative if Sensate Focus is not proceeding quickly enough. This can be done by suggesting alterations such as the use of lotion to vary the sensations or other modifications to help clients learn the skills they need before they can proceed.

Ticklishness

Because ticklishness is a reflexive reaction, it is often experienced as a challenge during initial sessions. Clients are reminded that ticklishness is a response we can rarely directly produce ourselves, and may be triggered by understandable anxiety when being touched by the partner. They are reassured that it is nothing to be embarrassed about and that it will diminish with Sensate Focus experience. Ticklishness that continues across touching opportunities can also suggest more complex and significant anxieties. Sometimes these can be severe and distressing, and may be associated with a history of relentlessly and even forcefully and relentlessly being tickled as a child.

The most frequent suggestion is to employ handriding, either removing the partner's hand or placing the ticklish person's hand under or over the partner's hand and move the Toucher's hand away in a more specific fashion in order to gain a greater sense of control. In some instances, such as feet ticklishness, the Toucher is asked to avoid that body area with the possibility of returning at a later time.

Feeling *Nothing*

Not infrequently, clients will return from Sensate Focus sessions reporting that they felt *nothing*. Just as with feeling bored with or constrained by Sensate Focus, this often means that they are still expecting to feel aroused and responsive, despite therapists' assurance that this is not the goal. This becomes diagnostic of a performance-oriented approach and serves as a teaching opportunity.

Feeling nothing may also be an indication of possible sexual trauma and dissociation, or it can point to other concerns such as damaged nerve conduction from illness, medication, or treatment. Additionally, it can signify a client's coming to therapy not to actually improve the sexual relationship. Instead, the client may be coming for therapy with a motivation to prove the sexual relationship is toxic or irretrievably broken, or there may be an ongoing affair or alternative sexual interest. Although every effort is made to identify these barriers during initial sessions, it is sometimes possible to do so only as problems surface in association with Sensate Focus suggestions.

The *feeling nothing* assertion is often best handled by asking the client to describe the sensation of their hands on the chair or their buttocks on the couch on which they are sitting. When they answer along the lines of, "It feels hard," the therapist reiterates that this is exactly the non-evaluative, sensory-oriented attitude that is being sought in the Sensate Focus experiences.

Sexual Frustration

Masters and Johnson's original suggestion that couples refrain from sexual release both during and apart from Sensate Focus sessions, and also that they not self-stimulate to orgasm, was aimed at allowing sexual tension to build in a non-demand way. It takes advantage of the principle that sex is a natural function and, therefore, the more that desire or arousal is *not* the goal, the more likely it is to occur. However, as the complexity of the Sensate Focus suggestions increases and begins to involve additional parts of the body, the sexual tension may also increase, and this may become a significant distraction.

Couples are encouraged to allow arousal to develop as any other emotion, and to lie next to each other for several minutes after the Sensate Focus session ends to see if the arousal will dissipate. If it does not, one or both clients may indicate their desire for physical release. However, this *follows* Sensate Focus and a period of time of lying next to each other or taking a break. As suggested previously, while one of the options is for the partner to provide manual release, the other two involve the person's requesting release to self-stimulate either by him or herself, or to self-stimulate in the presence of the partner while the partner holds the person seeking release. In any case, it is the *partner* who makes the decision about how the release takes place. A simple technique for handling release if both partners request it is to first provide release for the person who asked first, and then provide release for the person who asked subsequently.

The partner's choosing the type of release as the couple lies next to each other after Sensate Focus is particularly helpful when therapy takes place in a less intensive format. When Sensate Focus is associated with a longer-term outpatient format, it may also be productive to suggest clients engage in sexual activities if they feel the need as long as: these activities take place at an entirely different time, separate from the Sensate Focus opportunities; the partners are clear about the intent; and they are realistic about progress. Clients are still enjoined to have release apart from the touching sessions as infrequently as possible in order to foster higher levels of sexual tension.

Confusion About, and Difficulties With, Concepts and Instructions

Many of the attitudes and concepts of Sensate Focus are so different from the cultural scripts with which clients are raised, that confusions are likely. Sex as a natural function is a concept that is particularly difficult for many clients to apply especially when it comes to the notion that sexual responsiveness cannot be consciously produced. Often they have succeeded in most aspects of their lives by pouring conscious effort into whatever they have done. It may be difficult for them to embrace the idea that working hard at sexual response never works.

It may also be helpful to follow up verbal Sensate Focus instructions with a demonstration in the therapy office of the way in which to touch, especially for anxious clients. This is especially true for anxious clients. This is accomplished by having them use their hands to touch the chair or couch on which they are sitting and reporting about the touch sensations they experience. The instructions and touch demonstration can also be followed by giving clients a written instruction guide (see Appendix B).

When these strategies fail, ongoing confusion about the concepts and instructions may represent individual or partner dynamics of a more severe psychological nature. These may require additional professional expertise such as separate and intensive individual or couples therapy or a medication consultation as in the case of a client with obsessive-compulsive disorder.

Going Further Than Suggested on a Regular Basis

It is to be expected that clients who have experienced the build-up of sexual tension from repeated Sensate Focus may be spontaneously orgasmic during the touching as part and parcel of natural, sexual functioning. However, there are some couples that repeatedly and seemingly intentionally go beyond the current suggestions for Sensate Focus. They may even seek orgasmic release on a regular basis and as each successive touching opportunity is introduced, or may move on to intercourse repeatedly before this is encouraged. The usual intervention is to reiterate the concern about returning to goal-oriented expectations, a return which may reduce the opportunity for success in treatment. Sometimes the push for intercourse or orgasm is diagnostic of one partner's pressuring the other, of sexual compulsivity, of a personality disorder, or of a lack of sufficient education. All this is grist for the therapeutic mill.

Chapter 9: Diverse Populations With Psychological and Physical Concerns

If the common and expected problems described in the last chapter persist beyond the early stages of Sensate Focus, they may be indicative of more significant psychological or physical issues that require additional assessment and intervention. In fact, if some of these are evident during the history-taking, they may need to be addressed prior to or at the same time as the implementation of Sensate Focus. What follows are some psychological and physical concerns and the modifications for them that may be helpful or necessary.

Anxiety, Depression, Mood Disorders, or Psychosis

Presentation

The chances are high that clinicians will have clients presenting for sex therapy who are experiencing diagnosable Anxiety, Depressive, Bipolar, or Psychotic Disorders. We are not referring to occasional or everyday concerns, dysthymia, mood shifts, or unusual thoughts but rather psychological distress that meets formal criteria. Some have suggested that the sex therapy field is overrepresented with these types of clients. For example, the chances of suffering from decreased sexual interest is at least two times as great in women between 40 and 80 when formally diagnosed with a Depressive Disorder (Laumann et al., 2005). These concerns may have a significant impact on the development and maintenance of the sexual dysfunction, or they stand a good chance of impeding Sensate Focus progress if left untreated, or both.

Specific Treatment Modifications of Sensate Focus for Clients with Psychological Concerns

While implementing Sensate Focus is not impossible in instances of clinically diagnosable psychological disorders, it is most effective when done with the use of appropriate medications in consultation with clients' physicians. Additionally, adjunct therapy is often required before or at the same time as sex therapy and Sensate Focus. We must remember that almost all sex therapists have been trained originally and primarily in a mental health or medical field that is more generalized. This prepares them to work with clients encountering a variety of psychological issues, and also with couples' relationship concerns. Therefore, they are usually skilled at helping individuals and couples work on significant non-sexual problems either before or during sex therapy and the implementation of Sensate Focus, and either in individual sessions or in conjoint therapy. Another important point to emphasize is that sex therapy and Sensate Focus almost always include working with as many individual and couples issues as is necessary in order to resolve the sexual dysfunction. If the sex therapist does not feel skillful working with individual's or couples' diagnosable, non-sexual problems, he or she may want to refer clients to another therapist before or during Sensate Focus.

When it comes to working with significant psychological issues, we have also found it helpful to use cognitive-behavioral therapy (CBT) in separate sessions or as part of the couples and sex therapy sessions. Perhaps this is because Sensate Focus inside the bedroom is a variation of CBT outside of the bedroom, as we have suggested. When clients are directed to take note of their distractions (such as "I *should* get aroused") and then refocus their attention away from these distractions and onto sensations, they are, in fact, engaging in CBT. The essence of cognitive-behavior therapy is to recognize anxiety-provoking, unproductive, and irrational thoughts, attitudes, and experiences, and then to redirect attention onto something reliable that has a greater likelihood of evoking calming and more productive emotions and behaviors. Sensate Focus can be used as a formal, cognitive-behavioral management strategy, in and of itself, to assist clients with handling even their non-sexual-related anxiety and depressive concerns. The fear- and mood-alleviating powers of Sensate Focus can be remarkable for psychological issues that have little or nothing to do with sexual responsiveness but that, when alleviated, can help with the sexuality concerns.

However, clients with diagnosable psychological disorders can also be trained to use CBT outside of the bedroom to manage their non-sexual concerns in the more traditional way. In this case, they learn how to redirect their attention away from demand-oriented thoughts (such as, "I *should* feel a certain way") to more productive and rational beliefs (e.g., "I *wish* I could feel a certain way"). This helps the clients cultivate more productive thoughts, emotions, and behaviors outside of the bedroom in general, all of which also limits the negative effects of clients' individual psychological issues on Sensate Focus activities inside the bedroom. Again, this can be done either with both partners present or with the symptomatic partner in individual therapy.

Difficult or Challenging Clients
Presentation
As clinicians, most of us have experienced a difficult client or client couple. There is no substitute for good supervision and training in working with this population. These individuals and their partners often have issues with attachment, control, defensiveness, anger, empathy, helplessness, and characterological resistances that create challenges for the therapist. Sex therapists working with Sensate Focus suggestions are among these clinicians.

Specific Treatment Modifications of Sensate Focus for Challenging Clients
The single most helpful approach we have found for working with challenging clients who resist guidance is asking them what *they* would suggest doing with the Sensate Focus suggestions. In other words, we go with the resistance, even saying directly, "What would you suggest?" or "Why don't we try it your way?" For example, one of us recently had a case of DE in which the client was an extremely intelligent but reserved scientist and his partner an animated corporate executive. The client with DE resisted the scheduled touching sessions. He insisted the sessions should happen spontaneously. So the clinician,

after numerous but futile attempts to frame the scheduled sessions in therapeutic terms, invited the client into the planning process by suggesting, "Let's do it the way you have in mind." The idea here was that the least that would happen would be that the client had a legitimate approach and that the most that would happen would be that both partners would recognize the value of the scheduled approach. After one week of unstructured spontaneity, the client returned to the therapy session and, apparently forgetting that he had insisted on approaching the sessions informally, reported that he had come to a new conclusion: he thought what really needed to happen was to schedule the sessions at an appointed time. It turned into a win-win situation: the client was happy; the partner was pleased with the client's obvious investment in the therapeutic process; and the paradoxical injunction had worked well.

In a case of ED, the client was vigorously resisting the notion that he could not make himself have an erection and intercourse. Every time he engaged in Sensate Focus and had an erection, he would rush intercourse and, needless to say, lose his erection. After becoming concerned for the client's obvious discouragement, the clinician suggested that he consciously *will* himself an erection and insert each time. In very short order, the client subjectively experienced how unproductive this approach was and from then on honored the therapeutic suggestions.

Sometimes clients find the conjoint therapy too intense. They have trouble tolerating it despite all therapeutic and partner attempts to validate their perspective and support them in continuing. Granting the client a reprieve from couples therapy may be very helpful. Seeing them for a few individual sessions may be productive as they may find relief in being able to speak more openly without the partner being present.

In severe cases, the clinician may find it most beneficial to refer these clients to another therapist who specializes in dealing with challenging client issues. It might also be helpful to them to refer them to a specialized group such as one that offers Dialectical Behavior Therapy. It is usually advisable to proceed with Sensate Focus only after significant progress has been made in these other clinical settings. In more moderate cases, adjunct treatment of this nature can be used at the same time as sex therapy and Sensate Focus.

Substance Abuse

Clinicians don't hold a candle to the power of chemicals and, therefore, they shouldn't even try. Researchers in the field (Jensen, 1984) suggest that a useful rule of thumb is that someone who is alcohol or drug dependent should be sober for at least six months prior to the initiation of sex therapy.

In the meantime, what is most important is that clients participate in a recovery program, and it may be helpful for the clients to participate in individual and/or couples therapy to address the issues associated with the substance abuse and recovery from it, and to work on relationship and communication skills. Fostering greater intimacy outside of the bedroom, including the improvement of verbal communication skills and techniques for touching in sensual ways that do not lead to sexual activity, can be very helpful.

Sexual Trauma Survivors

There is probably no other historical antecedent that more often contributes to sexual difficulties for both men and women than sexual trauma. Sexual trauma may be a factor in issues related to body image, sexual orientation, gender identity, sexual risk-taking, sexual aversion, compulsive or out of control sexual behavior, desire, arousal, orgasmic, and pain difficulties, among others. Sexual trauma is especially influential if there has been recurrent childhood experience of sexual abuse by a close family member, extended family member, or trusted adult where the child perceives a lack of support and protection by caretakers (Finkelhor & Browne, 1985; Briere & Runtz, 1988; Weiner, 1988; Maltz, 2012; Courtois, 2016). Not only may these experiences permeate the survivors' sexuality but they also may impact attachment and trust and attempts to combine sexuality and intimacy. Unwanted or traumatic sexual experiences may also contribute to the development of other mental health and substance abuse problems including Post-Traumatic Stress Disorder (PTSD) and Dissociative Disorders. Not everyone who experiences sexual abuse suffers from PTSD, but it appears to be the case that those who do, often become our clients seeking sex therapy.

Presentation

Survivors may be of any gender, sexual orientation, gender identification, race, socio-economic class, nationality, or religious background. Clients who come to us for lack of desire or other sexual concerns may have experienced past sexual trauma including child sexual abuse, rape, or multiple incidents of non-consensual sex that they may not even have labeled as such. Most sexual trauma survivors are aware these experiences took place but may have minimized their impact. Others have sought help before, believe they have worked through the impact, and feel ready to move on to reclaim their sexuality for themselves and their partners, only to discover that the issues are not quite resolved. In some circumstances, clients have dissociated completely or partially from the events, and only their body tells the story.

Quite often, both partners report no problem with sexual expression during the early stages of their relationship. However, they may begin to experience sexual difficulties when they dedicate themselves to a relationship, whether this begins when they move in together or become formally committed. The combination of sexuality and intimacy may be overwhelmingly triggering, especially if the perpetrator was someone close to the victim. Other situations that may elicit disruptive symptoms (e.g., nightmares, flashbacks, or emotional numbing) include confronting a trigger such as the death of the perpetrator or a child who is the age they were at the time of their abuse.

Specific Treatment Modifications of Sensate Focus for Trauma Survivors: Trauma-Informed Approaches

Nowhere is the diagnostic power of Sensate Focus more evident than when working with traumatized clients. Sensate Focus can help uncover triggers and teach skills to manage reactions, thoughts, associations, and negative defenses associated with the trauma. However, each client must decide for him- or herself to take the journey into sexual healing.

Informed Approaches

Before introducing Sensate Focus it must be clear that the survivor is not currently in a dangerous or abusive relationship, and that the partner is genuinely interested in working with the survivor in therapy. The survivor must also not be under pressure from the partner or the therapist to engage in sex therapy. Survivors often feel guilty that their partners have to deal with the sexual consequences of their abuse history. However, it is not sufficient for survivors to begin sex therapy because they care deeply for their partners and consider it insensitive and unloving of them not to resolve the sexual problems. Survivors must be self-motivated ("I want this for me") or they may be replicating their victimization, albeit in well-intended fashion.

Empowerment

A primary approach when using Sensate Focus in a trauma-informed context is empowerment of the survivor. This includes: educating survivors about the symptoms and adaptive tools they utilized to cope; encouraging them to take charge of the process of learning to touch and be touched while remaining present; and learning how to become physically and emotionally comfortable with their bodies and sexual responses.

Triggers

Taking a thorough sexual history, as always, is critical. This includes identifying what clients recall about the abuse, clarifying what their coping strategies have been and are now, identifying triggers in the present, and assessing the nature, quality, and efficacy of their management strategies. Triggers are stimuli that bring about essentially reflexive, almost automatic protective reactions. These reflexive responses amount to fight, flight, or freeze. They often seem confusing to survivors, or may be considered over reactions to the current situation (Van der Kolk, 2014; Cohn, 2011). As each trigger is identified and processed, the survivor becomes more and more in charge of his or her body in the present moment.

Individual Sessions

Sensate Focus alternates between individual processing and couples work as needed. When the emphasis is on individual work with the survivor, the partner is also seen intermittently to address his or her feelings and needs. Many partners report feeling helpless and confused about the reasons the survivor cannot perceive them as distinct from the perpetrator(s), and move beyond the traumatic experiences. They often need the therapist's support as much as the survivor.

Couple Sessions

When clients are highly anxious or phobic, or when they are anxious about proceeding with more traditional Sensate Focus suggestions, the partner who is the survivor is initially invited to take charge of the pacing of the touching sessions, and the development of the hierarchy of touching. Clients can begin the sessions fully or partially clothed. They may choose to have the session in some place other than the bedroom, like on a living room couch or in some other area of the house where they feel more comfortable. They can begin with touching the hand. They may touch their partner without having the partner touch them. They may have only their breasts touched and not their genitals, or vice versa. The survivor is also in charge of when the touching occurs and how long it lasts. In order to feel more in control, the survivor may liberally use handriding to move the partner's hand away, or place his or her hand under or over the partner's hand. The survivor can also use a code word to communicate anxiety and to signal the need for a change in the action. Other techniques for reducing anxiety and the likelihood of dissociating include breathing, keeping eyes open, asking the partner to keep eyes closed, and using positive self-talk (thinking things such as, "This is something for me"). Also the survivor may subsequently use positive handriding to communicate the way in which he or she is interested in being touched.

As with all Sensate Focus suggestions, whatever is problematic will arise and then be processed during the therapy sessions. The story is always being told. As clinicians, we just have to listen. For example, a client who was able to touch for herself, to focus on sensations, and to bring herself back from distractions was moving along with manageable anxiety until her partner touched her inner thigh and she felt slight arousal. This triggered a panic reaction, and she stopped the touching session as suggested. She requested her partner hold her in silence. We subsequently processed a memory related to experiencing this same action during childhood abuse. She recalled she had had an unwanted orgasm that produced feelings of shame, guilt, and powerlessness. Once the association was identified and addressed in individual therapy the client was able to continue with Sensate Focus and couple work by using handriding with her partner on her inner leg, under her own direction, and for increased periods of time. She was eventually able to allow herself to experience feelings of arousal and orgasm without triggering her panic.

Other Techniques

Many clinicians have contributed to our work with trauma survivors and their partners in both Gay and straight relationships (Haines, 2007; Herman, 1997; Courtois, 2016). Wendy Maltz (2012) has created a multitude of exercises for survivors and their partners to relearn touch. These include the practice of holding, listening to the partner's heartbeat, playful contact, body drawing, and massage, among others. The emphasis in these exercises is on building safety, initiating and guiding contact, creating body awareness and, ultimately allowing pleasure. Maltz has also contributed to our suggestions for handling unwanted sexual fantasies and processing shameful secrets.

Other clinicians have made innovative use of a complete body map. Red, yellow, and green colors are used to highlight areas of the body with neutral or negative charges. These maps are used to identify triggering parts of the body, and they are shared with partners (Zoldrod, 2015).

Exposure-based techniques have been applied to the treatment of sexual trauma (Lee, Gavriel, Drummond, Richards, & Greenwald, 2002). Our preference is to process trauma using Eye Movement Desensitization and Reprocessing (EMDR) (Edmond, 1999; Pillai-Friedman, 2010; Shapiro, 2001). Other clinicians emphasize attachment theory, emotionally focused therapies, somatically based techniques, and neurofeedback (Fisher, 2014; Robbins, 2000). These can all be used in conjunction with Sensate Focus. Still others help survivors and their partners move towards healing by interweaving Sensate Focus with dream journaling and also with additional mindfulness exercises (Brotto, Seal, & Rellini, 2012).

Spectrum and Other Developmental Issues

As we are increasingly seeing couples in which one or both individuals have been diagnosed with Spectrum Disorders, we decided to touch on this subject. Unfortunately, few procedural suggestions for Sensate Focus have been developed as yet to address their special circumstances.

Psychological and Physical Concerns

Presentation

While each Spectrum client is a separate individual and deserves an individualized assessment, there are common areas known to create challenges. These include: communication difficulties; difficulties understanding the sexual and emotional needs of the partner; problems adapting to change and handling stress; and tactile and other sensory sensitivities. These often pose concerns for the relationship both inside and outside of the bedroom. In working with couples in which one is diagnosed as being on the Autistic Spectrum (AS) and the other is not (NT, or *neurotypical*), it may be especially difficult for the AS client to recognize the partner's need for emotional intimacy prior to the partner's being interested in sex. An additional factor may be the AS partner's need for concrete instruction around affection and sexual expression.

Specific Treatment Modifications of Sensate Focus for Spectrum Clients

Individuals with Spectrum Disorders may have differences in sensory perception including *under* sensitivity and *over* sensitivity that vary from moment to moment. Whether the sensitivity is to auditory, olfactory, or tactile sensations, the therapist must devise a strategy that works for the couple. For example, a body suit that limits the possibility of overstimulation during touching or sexual encounters is now available. There is also a helpful technique, the use of *a body map* created by Raymond Sealove (R. Sealove, personal communication, September 6, 2012). This can help to illustrate particularly sensitive areas.

As many AS clients have a strong need for structure, routine, and sameness, Sensate Focus suggestions can be a welcome addition to their repertoire. Having the Touchee move the Toucher's hand away to protect the Toucher from doing anything psychologically or physically uncomfortable is often welcomed and very helpful. Similarly, including positive handriding to indicate interest engenders a stronger sense of confidence and safety while engaging in Sensate Focus.

Physical Challenges: Aging, Illness, and Disabilities

There has been much research conducted on Sensate Focus and people who are aging (Agronin, 2014; Price, 2015; Shaw, 2014), who experience medical problems (Gallo-Silver, 2000; Jindal & Jindal, 2010; Sanders & Sprenkle, 1980), and who have disabilities (Bell, Toplis, and Espie, 1999; Melby, 2011). Sensate Focus is regarded as integral to sex therapy for these couples (Enzlin, 2014; Mona, Syme, & Cameron, 2014). There are a number of modifications of Sensate Focus that are helpful for people confronting physical challenges. Resources supporting these modifications abound (Agronin, 2014; Auteri, 2014; Castleman, 2011, 2012; McCarthy, 2005; Price, 2015; Shaw, 2014).

Noted sexologist Mitchell Tepper, Ph.D., (2000; 2015) suggests that often it is the way in which people think about touching and sex that plays a vital role in working with physically challenged couples. Perhaps there is no other area where beliefs about touching and sex have a greater negative impact on the implementation of Sensate Focus.

Psycho-Education About Beliefs

Whether the challenges are the result of aging, illness, or disability, medical and physical constraints pose additional difficulties for engaging in Sensate Focus. However, these difficulties are often primarily associated with how clients think about sex, Sensate Focus, and physical challenges in general. While there is no question that the most important goal of Sensate Focus with aging, chronically ill, or disabled couples is to minimize pain and to maximize comfort and mobility, the next most important goal is to provide education and counseling that challenges their thought patterns and limiting beliefs. The psycho-education and counseling that accompanies the use of Sensate Focus with aging, and medically and physically challenged people may be perhaps best be summarized as helping couples reframe their apparent encumbrances as, in fact, opportunities for adaptation.

My Sex Life is Over!

The most significant belief that has a negative impact on sex therapy is that one's sex life is over as one ages or encounters a physical limitation. By virtue of the fact that sex is a natural function, just about everyone continues to respond sexually no matter what physical constraints exist. For example, few people are aware of the fact that, despite a decline in sexual responsivity as the aging process occurs, over two-thirds of individuals 57–64, between one- and two-thirds of individuals 65–74, and between one-fifth and one-third of individuals 75–85 are sexually active (Lindau et al., 2007). Fifty-four percent of the oldest active partners engage in some type of sexual activity two-three times a month, and 23% do so at least once a week. The conclusion that intimate physical contact with self and others has come to an end when aging or other physical or medical distresses occur robs us of the known medical and psychological benefits of touching and, ultimately, of more functional and meaningful sex.

If It's Different, It's No Good

A second belief that hinders meaningful sexual contact is the notion that touching is not the same when medical constraints are involved; therefore, if the touch does not lead to intercourse, then sex is not as meaningful. However, different doesn't mean non-existent or impossible! The most useful attitude is to focus *not on what cannot be done* but *on what* can *be done*! Michael Metz and Barry McCarthy (2012) have recently written about what they refer to as the *Good Enough Sex Model.* They suggest that sexual satisfaction can actually increase as couples age. Just as you cannot run around the block when you are 78 the way you could when you were 18 doesn't mean you cannot walk around it. The advantage may be that you notice and can savor the proverbial flowers that you would otherwise have missed.

I Am Not Normal

A third belief that can interfere with sexuality in physically challenged individuals is the sense that they are not *normal*, whatever that might mean to them. This is associated with the previous belief that because things have changed and are different, they are (the individual is) abnormal. To be older, ill, or disabled is not abnormal. Educating people about this, and helping them appreciate what their body has to offer, is a very important aspect of sex therapy and Sensate Focus. It helps them explore and experiment with what *does* work for them rather than with what they think *should* work for them.

Psychological and Physical Concerns

If It's Not Spontaneous, It's Pointless

A fourth belief about sexuality that poses an obstacle to sex when there are physical or medical constraints is the notion that if touch is not spontaneous, it is pointless. More careful orchestrating of Sensate Focus may become increasingly important when experiencing age- or medically-related challenges. However, spontaneity and meaningful touching sessions are not one and the same thing. In fact, it could be argued that *the importance of spontaneous touching is one of the most overrated aspects of intimate connections*, particularly in the context of a long-term relationship. As we have suggested, to have a successful party, one must plan ahead. That doesn't mean anything about the spontaneity that may happen once the party is underway.

Technical and Logistical Modifications

In addition to psycho-education about the beliefs that negatively impact sex in these populations, there are technical and logistical changes in the touching opportunities that may help Sensate Focus become more helpful to couples with physical restrictions.

Furniture, Pillows, and Other Equipment

There are a number of companies that manufacture furniture and other equipment that can be extremely useful in providing support and assistance. For example, Liberator (www.liberator.com) and Loving Angles (www1.loving-angles.com) design wedges, ramps, furniture, hard cushions, and other supportive devices that are extremely helpful for couples experiencing back, limb, neck, and other concerns. For individuals with movement difficulties, using a bed ladder may be valuable for turning in the bed. For couples who would benefit from the astride person's being elevated more highly above the partner who is lying down, firm cushions or pillows placed under the astride person's lower legs is critical.

Other Helpful Adjuncts

Where pelvic pain is experienced, partners may prefer to use an adult toy, such as a dildo, for insertion. This allows for a greater sense of control with depth of insertion or the speed of motion. Cock rings often assist men experiencing engorgement concerns. Where neurological or other medical conditions are involved, a vibrator may make sensations more vivid and intense. Non-oil based lubricants and gels for both women and men may enhance comfort with physical contact.

Positions

Many aging, chronically ill, and physically challenged women prefer sitting in front of their partners when breasts and genitals are on limits rather than lying down on their backs, in between the partners' legs. Women who have had pelvic surgery or experience distress may want to assume the female astride position more often. They may want to be more in control of insertion in order to precisely manage the depth of penetration. Clients with hip difficulties may prefer positions in which their legs are not spread open but rather where they are lying on their sides and approached from behind.

Clothing

Body image in this population may more often be the source of distress. For example, a woman who has undergone a mastectomy may be self-conscious and may find it easier, particularly in the early stages of Sensate Focus, to keep on a bra, a loose fitting nightgown, or lingerie to minimize body image distractions.

Timing

Scheduling Sensate Focus when clients are not fatigued or in physical distress, when their medications have positive rather than negative effects, or before or after activities like bowel or bladder care, can improve the ability to focus on sensations and to neutralize distracting anxieties. Optimizing environmental cues (lighting and temperature), psychological cues (mood, self-confidence), and interpersonal connection (productive verbal and non-verbal communication beforehand), can further facilitate effective sensory focusing.

Chapter 10: Sensate Focus 1 and 2

The initial Sensate Focus suggestions are just that, the initial suggestions. We have been referring to these as Sensate Focus 1. The emphasis has been on psycho-education, cognitive-behavioral patterns, affect management, unproductive relationship dynamics, and mindfulness techniques when working with individuals or couples who present with sexual dysfunctions. However, alleviating sexual dysfunctions is not all there is to sex therapy in general and Sensate Focus in particular. Even when individuals and couples ostensibly come in to address their dysfunctions, their ultimate goal is often improving the overall satisfaction of their relationship. They want more emotional closeness, greater intimacy, better sensual communication, and more engaging sexual experiences. This is where Sensate Focus 2 comes in.

Moving From Sexual Dysfunction to Sexual Enrichment: Sensate Focus 2

Sensate Focus 2 emphasizes the *enrichment*, *enhancement*, or *optimization* of sexual relationships rather than just the resolution of sexual dysfunction. Peggy Kleinplatz has spearheaded sexual optimization, studying couples that report having *great sex*. The characteristics she has identified as typifying sexual optimization, what we refer to as Sensate Focus 2, suggest overlaps with Sensate Focus 1. In fact, Sensate Focus 2 incorporates two of the most salient characteristics of Sensate Focus 1, namely, being mindfully *present* and being *authentic*. With regard to the first, "The most predominant and fully articulated characteristic ... [is] being 'fully present' and 'totally absorbed in the moment'" (Kleinplatz & Ménard, 2007, p. 73). With regard to authenticity, the emphasis is on each partner's absorption in, candor with, and expression of his or her own experience: "Being present [is] inextricably linked for most participants with a second component of being themselves ... and being relentlessly honest with themselves."

However, Sensate Focus 2 moves beyond mindful self-focus that encourages developing an authentic relationship with one's own sensuality. The spotlight is increasingly on "feeling free to be themselves *with* their partners" (Kleinplatz & Ménard, 2007, p. 73, emphasis added). Now we begin to highlight the interaction *between* the partners rather than what is happening with each individual client. More and more attention is paid to their *emotional connection*, their *sexual and erotic intimacy*, and their *communication*.

Intense emotional connection involves heightened engagement with one another. Sexual and erotic intimacy includes the willingness to be vulnerable and to surrender, trusting that

10.1
Sensate Focus 2

the partner will respond with care and generosity. Communication is associated with both the verbal and non-verbal exchange of information, and also with the sounds and vocalizations that each partner experiences as stimulating and ultimately arousing. In our experience it is the qualities of intense emotional connection, vulnerability, surrender, and communication that most couples hope to bring to, or access within, their relationship when they come for

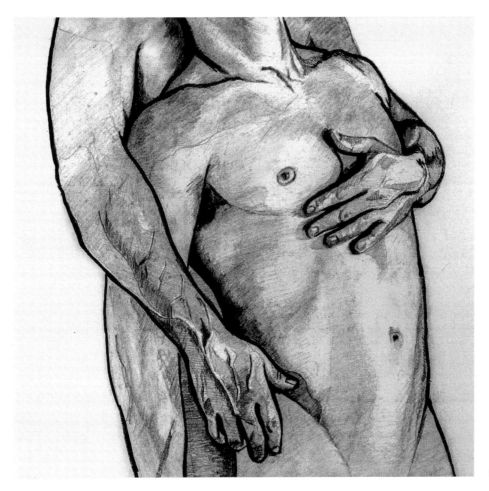

10.2
Sensate Focus 2

sex therapy. This is regardless of whether their original goal is to resolve a sexual dysfunction or optimize their sexual intimacy.

However, there is one additional characteristic of Sensate Focus 2 that is perhaps even more important than these relationship enhancements. Clients do not talk about it directly, perhaps because it crosses over into the realm of indescribable experience. However, over the years we have come to appreciate it as the ultimate, if unspoken, goal of those who come in for sex therapy. Kleinplatz refers to this as *transcendence.* It goes by many names, none of which do it justice: "'peak experience,' ... 'magical experiences,' and 'spirituality' ... 'a portal to an alternate reality' ... 'expansive and enlightening' ... 'it leaves you bigger than you were before' ... 'flashes of illumination' ... 'It [is] revelatory – an epiphany'" (Kleinplatz & Ménard, 2007, pp. 75–76). Noted analyst James Hollis refers to it as "the god to be found in sexuality" and suggests that clients who want to enrich their sexual lives "follow what [the poet] Rilke called the dark 'river god of the blood' ... The higher power are powers, indeed, but so are the lower ones ... [and] sexuality, the dark river god of the blood, is sacred" (1998, pp. 91–92). This spiritual or transcendent dimension of sexuality requires entering into the radically self-focused mindset of Sensate Focus 1 but this time through a deeply sensorial, sensual, and emotional relationship with the partner that characterizes Sensate Focus 2. This is when absorption *in* the sensations moves into absorption *by* the sensations and ultimately into an altered state of consciousness that is transcendent sexual responsiveness to which we refer in Chapter 2 (Why is Sensate Focus Based on Touch?). This sensorial, sensual, sexual, emotional, and relational integration leads not only to the enlargement of each partner but also to the enlarged intimate connection between the partners.

Techniques for Optimizing Sexual Intimacy and Interaction

Suggestions to enhance sexual satisfaction and enrich intimate communication will be the subject of subsequent publications. But a brief mention of some of these techniques is helpful if only to distinguish them from those used in Sensate Focus 1. A summary of Sensate Focus approaches also is important to re-emphasize the main goal of this *Illustrated Manual*, namely, to clarify the purpose of Sensate Focus 1 as mindfully self-focused touching.

Sensate Focus 2 suggestions incorporate more information between partners about what each prefers sensorally, sensually, and sexually (Weiner & Avery-Clark, 2014). In the non-verbal arena, Sensate Focus 2 emphasizes positive handriding to a much greater extent. The Touchee is increasingly encouraged to place his/her hand on top of or beneath the Toucher's hand and to direct the Toucher's hand *towards areas that the Touchee finds not only interesting* (in terms of vivid tactile sensations) but also *arousing, pleasurable, and enjoyable*. Words of this evaluative, emotional nature are increasingly woven into the fabric of the Sensate Focus therapy sessions. This is because by the time they reach Sensate Focus 2, most couples are aware of the difference between sensations and emotions like arousal and pleasure, and they know how to refocus on these sensations if and when they have difficulty staying focused on emotions without becoming goal-oriented.

Additionally, direct verbal communication is increasingly encouraged as partners are invited to openly express more subtle preferences during the touching sessions. Their communication outside of the bedroom can also become a greater focus as the interaction between what goes on inside and outside of the bedroom is increasingly taken into account.

Back in the bedroom, or wherever the touching experiences are taking place, couples are encouraged to expand their emotional connection, intimacy, and communication through experimenting with a wider variety of activities and adjuncts. For example, clients are invited to read material to one another they find arousing, and to share visual images. They are emboldened to create fantasy scenarios and games, and they can act these out if it is of interest to them and helpful for them. They are urged to incorporate toys and vibrators into their play together with other accessories such as cock rings, dildos, and any other accouterments they might have thought about but never actually included. These activities will not be of interest to, or comfortable for, everyone. Couples are invited to explore them at least once if they are so inclined, or not, all with the goal of discovering what is mutually engaging.

The Relation Between Sensate Focus 1 and 2

Even when Sensate Focus 2 has been initiated, the skills developed during Sensate Focus 1 still serve a purpose. Clients are reminded that should they encounter difficulty, should they find themselves slipping back into a demand orientation expecting desire, arousal, or orgasm, or should they experience their partner's appearing to regress, they can redirect their attention back to the touch sensations for their own interest in order to ground themselves once again in something reliable. At any point couples might find themselves having renewed concerns and so it is important that clinicians normalize this pattern. Even something so simple as going a week without any physical contact may be enough for old habits of goal orientation and anxiety to slip back into the touching and make it seem uncomfortable and even awkward. Returning to a couple of sessions of Sensate Focus 1 may bring them back to the ease with which they were having physical contact previously.

However, the most important point about the relation between Sensate Focus 1 and 2 is that it is not possible to experience intense emotional connection, sexual and erotic intimacy, open communication, and inspiring transcendence without first knowing the basics of self-focused sensorial absorption. This is the foundation of all deeply meaningful sexual experiences. One could think of it this way: Would an introductory teacher put you in the same proverbial ring with a highly trained expert in the field? Would a boss count on you to handle a tricky professional negotiation if you were brand new to the job? More than likely you would be trained to master new and basic skills essential to your goal, and you would be assisted in unlearning problematic habits, all in an effort to ensure you succeed. It is the same with Sensate Focus 1. In order to dismantle the anxiety-engendering performance and demand distractions that contribute to sexual problems, clients must first learn how to manage these differently before they can move on to optimizing sexual involvement. In order to ground themselves once basic skills have been learned and enhancement is at hand, clients can return to foundational Sensate Focus 1 techniques whenever the expected regressions and difficulties resurface. And we tell them so!

Chapter 11: Conclusion

We began *Sensate Focus in Sex Therapy: The Illustrated Manual* by suggesting that we know a lot more about sex than we did half a century ago when Masters and Johnson began publishing their groundbreaking work on sexual functioning and sex therapy. After researching and writing this manual, we, ourselves, know a lot more about Sensate Focus than we did when we began. We have been impressed with the extent to which practitioners and researchers from a wide variety of fields have expanded on the original work of Masters and Johnson with a wide variety of clients from all sorts of populations. Their creativity and willingness to cultivate a fertile ground for the exchange of ideas across professional specializations is remarkable. Additionally, and despite our decades of training in and working with Sensate Focus as the foundation of our sex therapy practices, we were not aware of how many clinicians use and find effective this simple yet powerful technique while helping many different kinds of people who experience sexual dysfunctions. We have been humbled and delightfully surprised! We have also been rewarded to discover how many clinicians find Sensate Focus to be as effective a therapeutic approach as we do.

Writing this manual is the fulfillment of a mission that was initiated by Masters and Johnson's work when they promised to explain Sensate Focus in greater detail. For whatever reason, they left this promise unfulfilled, leading many people to tell us about the importance of writing the manual to clarify and codify Sensate Focus. This manual represents the first time Masters and Johnson's foundational techniques of Sensate Focus are described in such detail and are available to everyone. We hope the additions by others and the clarifications we present will stimulate researchers in the field to do additional research and breathe fresh ideas and best practices into our field.

Writing this *Illustrated Manual* represents the fulfillment of several other goals. When we began we were aware that the field of sexuality had been moving in a medicalized direction in large measure because of the development and proliferation of PDE-5 inhibitors. However, we really did not appreciate to what extent this had happened. We hope that we have been able to shine the spotlight back onto the *whole* field of sexual healing that includes not just what physicians, nurse practitioners, and physical therapists are doing but also what psychologists, social workers, educators, relationship therapists, sociologists, spiritual leaders, and stress management counselors have to offer. We anticipate a renewal of vitality in a multidisciplinary approach in which all these professionals proactively reach out to, confer with, and cross-train one another, so that we can all better serve our clients and

Conclusion

society with the important work we do. This is instead of merely paying lip service to what we know intellectually but so often do nothing about practically, namely, advancing the understanding that sexuality is so varied that to presume any one profession embodies everything there is to know about the field is to do the field in general, and our clients in particular, a tremendous disservice. Michael Perelman's erudite and elegantly constructed *Sexual Tipping Point®* model (2009) reminds us of the dynamic interaction between the constitutionally established capacity to respond in a sexual fashion (the natural function of sexual responsiveness) and the actual elicitation of that response by different kinds of stimulation that are influenced in an ongoing way by a wide variety of psychosocial-behavioral and cultural factors.

If we do not heed this need for an ardent multidisciplinary approach to working with sexual issues, we risk the fate of professions that have become so exclusive as to render themselves arcane and eventually irrelevant as a result.

> The world of intellectual possibilities has developed in unfathomable diversity. Infinitely long paths, paved with thousands of thick volumes, lead from one specialization to another. Soon no one will be able to walk down these paths anymore. And then only specialists will remain. More than ever we require … something capable of providing firm guidance.
>
> (Jung, 2009, p. 286, fn. 135)

The firmer guidance offered by a more complex and nuanced multidisciplinary approach to sexuality parallels one of our expressed reasons for writing this manual and that is to shine the spotlight back on the whole person as well as on the whole field. We are clearly big supporters of the need to honor and address the underlying physiological, natural responses before all other dimensions. Nonetheless, it is a rare client who comes to therapy solely to address biological concerns. Clients want to learn how to manage their own anxieties better, how to communicate with their partner more intimately, how to wrestle with values that no longer serve them well, and how to cope more efficiently with stresses in their daily lives. This is all in service to resolving sexual dysfunctions and improving sexual relationships. Addressing one or a couple of these aspects without respecting the influence of the others is like the blind touching the proverbial elephant: an appreciation for the entirety is forsaken in favor of a rigid adherence to myopic perspectives that lead to conflict and, in the case of sexologists, disservice to our clients.

As we worked on this manual, we were perplexed to discover that there are some who suggest that sex therapy, and Sensate Focus along with it, has little to offer as a unique specialty and that they are considered essentially passé. Needless to say, we would respectfully disagree. This puzzling perspective seems to parallel the movement of increasing medicalization of the field of sexuality. However, as is so often the case, there is strong evidence that the pendulum may be starting to swing the other way. There is an increasing awareness in the mental health and possibly even in the medical fields of the unique contributions made by sex therapists and clinicians who are comfortable providing sex education, information, and strategic interventions such as Sensate Focus.

We hope that this *Illustrated Manual* will stimulate a rebirth of interest in and appreciation for sex therapy in general and Sensate Focus in particular. Our hope dovetails with questions about the unique purview of sex therapy and Sensate Focus in that both have the potential for stimulating more evidence-based research in these areas, research that is sorely needed. For example, where is significant evidence to suggest who uses sex therapy and Sensate Focus? If professionals trained in only one health or mental health specialty represent the great majority of sex therapists and professionals who use Sensate Focus then maybe both health and mental health professionals can be subsumed under some one specialty and do not have much to offer in the way of unique therapy. Our experience has been quite different. We have been impressed with the fact that sex therapists and clinicians who use Sensate Focus come from divergent backgrounds including psychologists, social workers, psychiatrists, mental health counselors, marriage and family therapists, health personnel, physicians, nurse practitioners, physical therapists, and religious and spiritual counselors, to name some. This would suggest that there is something special that sex therapy and Sensate Focus have to offer that is not included in the training of a diverse number of health and mental health professions. Nonetheless, there is little in the way of evidence-based investigations to provide a firmer objective foundation for our experience.

Another rich area for research has to do with contentions we have often made throughout this manual. These include our claims that the specific way in which Sensate Focus rationale and instructions are presented, and the specific questions asked of clients in order to process Sensate Focus during the therapy sessions, have significant bearing on how well clients understand the concepts of Sensate Focus. We also contend that these have considerable influence on how willing clients are to carry out the suggestions, and how effectively they cultivate the attitudes and skills that are most productive for implementing it. But are these empirically the case? Precise data has yet to be gathered. We think it would be interesting and invaluable for significant investigations to be initiated to objectively assess these claims.

Yet one other fertile field of inquiry would be evaluating the modifications suggested for Sensate Focus with a diversity of populations. There is a dearth of methodologically sound research on this. Do the changes in Sensate Focus that we encourage and that have been suggested by other clinicians actually make a significant difference beyond these clinicians' reports? What precisely are the modifications to Sensate Focus that work best with different populations, and what new modifications are needed and can be created?

The whole question of the objective effectiveness of Sensate Focus in general continues to intrigue us. There have been few systematic studies into how well Sensate Focus works beyond experiential, anecdotal reports. What is the operationally defined effectiveness of Sensate Focus in the short term? How about in the long term?

These are but a few of the investigative questions that we hope readers will consider as the field of sex therapy and Sensate Focus develops even more creatively, productively, and inclusively. Our wish is that this expansion in research spearheads a more general resurgence of interest in, and appreciation for, sex therapy and Sensate Focus stimulated by this manual.

Two other points deserve emphasis. Throughout the preparation for and writing of this manual, we have been humbled repeatedly by the primalness and power of touch. We noted at the beginning that touch is the first sensory system to develop and arguably the most compelling. Recently there was a video posted in which a woman went into premature labor with twins, and was informed that the male twin had not lived through the delivery.

> I just grabbed the baby from the doctor, and unwrapped him, and ordered [my husband] to get his clothes off because I wanted him to get in bed with me because

Conclusion

> I wanted as much body heat around this baby as possible because he was cold and I wanted him to be warm and alive. We put his skin against my skin, and I just held him close to my heart. I moved his head so he would be able to hear my heart beating. And cried. And cried … So we are balling our eyes out and holding him, and then he started to move. We thought, "What? What's happening?" … We said, "Look, he's moving," and they said, "He's dying" … And we never let go of him. His skin was against mine for the entire time. And then he opened his eyes … and he grabbed [his father's] finger … He laid his head back down on my chest … And we realized it was because we had held him and he had the body heat … and that soft cocooning warmth … That's what had brought him back and had given him the time … to live!
>
> (Diamond, n.d., 1:10–3:13)

What more powerful testament to the life-giving energy of touch can there be? It is this energy that Sensate Focus harnesses, and the healing effect it can have on sexual responsivity in particular, and feelings of wellbeing and life in general, is remarkable.

Finally, perhaps the most professionally and personally meaningful reason we undertook publishing *Sensate Focus in Sex Therapy: The Illustrated Manual* (1975; 1987) is to remind all of us that fundamental to sex therapy and Sensate Focus is the beauty and humanity of sex. Helen Singer Kaplan did this some four decades ago by including illustrations in her *Illustrated Manual of Sex Therapy* (1975; 1987). We hope the drawings laced among the pages of this book will inspire and remind us why we do this work.

> Sexuality is the great mystery of our being, sensuality the first cog in our machinery. It stirs our whole being and makes it alive and joyful. All our dreams of beauty and nobility have their source here. Sensuality and sexuality constitute the essence of music, of painting, and of all the arts. All the desires of mankind revolve round this centre like moths round a flame. The sense of beauty and artistic feeling are only other dialects, other expressions. They signify nothing more than the sexual urge of mankind.
>
> (Jung, 1990, para. 332n)

Appendix A: Sexual Dysfunction: History-Taking for Sexual Distress, Adapted from Masters & Johnson Institute©

Linda Weiner, MSW, and
Constance Avery-Clark, PhD

I. Purpose of Taking the History
    A. To establish diagnosis
    B. To assess contributing and maintenance factors
    C. To assess who these partners are as individuals (style of thinking, biases, etc.)
    D. To tease out relationship strengths and weaknesses
    E. To determine views of therapy; therapist
    F. To plan appropriate intervention

II. Format
    A. Introductory remarks and review of procedures
        1. History-taking on partners and their relationship
        2. Psychological testing (as needed to diagnose Attention Deficit Hyperactivity Disorder, depression, etc.)
        3. Physical exams and laboratory work (as needed)
        4. Roundtable or sharing perceptions of problem/treatment plan
        5. Daily suggestions; processing
    B. Red flagging, or limited confidentiality
    C. Presenting problem and the client's perception of it
        1. Detail of the problem
        2. Onset and duration
        3. Manifestations (variability, consistency, trends)
        4. Coping strategies
        5. Feelings associated with the problems
        6. Attribution
        7. Impact of problem on relationship and individuals
        8. Attempts at remedy; effects, level of success
        9. Reason for entering therapy at this time
        10. Client and partner's commitment to therapy
        11. Therapy goals
    D. Present relationship
        1. Sexually (preferences, feelings, patterning, monogamy, etc.)
        2. Socially (friends, shared interests, etc.)
        3. Emotionally (complementary)

4. Interactions (communication patterns) especially concerning:
   a. Demonstrating affection
   b. Decision making
   c. Managing conflict (children, money, etc.)
   d. Initiating sexual activity
   e. Leisure and free time
5. Commitment

E. Development of present relationship
   1. Meeting
   2. Attraction
   3. Evolution of relationship

F. Family of origin/childhood
   1. Atmosphere
      a. Regarding nudity, physical modesty
      b. Bathroom and bedroom privacy
      c. Amount and type of discipline
   2. Parent's relationship
   3. Relationship between parents and children
   4. Birth order of and relationship between siblings
   5. Sexual interaction between siblings
   6. Sexual interaction among other family members
   7. Physical illness or disorders during childhood

G. Religious issues
   1. Specific religious/spiritual orientation
   2. Religious orthodoxy of family of origin
   3. Client's commitment at present
   4. Client's perception of religious background, current beliefs and their effects on:
      a. Attitudes towards self
      b. Attitudes towards sex

H. Career issues
   1. Perception of self in relation to employment/career
   2. Academic/professional/career ambitions
   3. Extent to which these have or have not been met – reasons – reactions
   4. Amount of time and energy expended in career activities

I. Sex history
   1. Sex play as a child
   2. Body exploration and stimulation
      a. When started
      b. Under what circumstances
      c. Techniques and how done (body position, precursors, fantasies)
      d. Results of exploration/stimulation
   3. Sexual information
      a. When and where did client first learn about sex?
      b. Knowledge regarding own body

4. Partner stimulation
    a. When first began and with whom
    b. Type of activity
    c. Reactions
5. First intercourse/insertion experience, as appropriate
    a. When occurred and associated expectations
    b. Details of event
    c. Attitudes and values at that time
    d. Reactions
6. Traumatic sexual events
    a. Incest, sexual abuse, or rape
    b. Coercion or physical abuse associated with sexual interaction
    c. Disturbing sexual encounters
    d. Extra-marital/extra-relational affairs
    e. Sexually transmitted infections
    f. Pregnancy scares and/or pregnancy terminations
7. Present attitudes towards sexual interaction
    a. What does client get out of it?
    b. Does client let partner know what he/she wants?
8. Present sexual response pattern
    a. Sexual orientation, gender identification
    b. Sexual interest or desire
    c. Sexual arousal (excitement to plateau-erection or lubrication)
    d. Orgasmic experience (plateau to orgasm-ejaculation or muscle contractions)
    e. Distractions and how these are handled
    f. Attitudes towards bodily secretions
    g. Masturbatory pattern
    h. Sexual fantasies
    i. Erotic turn-ons
J. Dating history
    1. When began and associated expectations
    2. Significant partners
    3. How did relationship end?
    4. Type and frequency of sexual activity
    5. Attraction
    6. Degree of emotional involvement
    7. Perceived consequences
K. Prior marital/committed relationship history
    1. Prior marriages/committed relationships
    2. The circumstances
    3. Attraction
    4. Reason for termination
    5. Types of sexual activity and response patterns

L.   Reproductive issues

1. Menstruation (for women)

    a. Preparation

    b. Onset

    c. Difficulties

    d. Use of tampons

2. Post-menopause (for women)

    a.   Onset

    b.   Difficulties

    c.   Hormone replacement therapy

3.   Contraception

    a.   Type

    b.   When started

    c.   Any type used with first intercourse?

    d.   Difficulties

    e.   Current method

    f.   Pregnancies

    g.   Scares premaritally/postmaritally

    h.   Abortions/terminations – complications?

    i.   Deliveries – complications?

    j.   Children

    k.   Planned?

    l.   Desired currently?

    m.   Pelvic/genital exam

    n.   First age

    o.   Reactions

    p.   Current reactions to pelvic exams

M.   Emotional issues (level of feelings: depth, lack of, distress with)

1.   Self

2.   The relationship

3.   Sexual issues

4.   Partner

5.   Sex roles

6.   Self-concept

    a.   Presently

    b.   Any changes especially in relation to body image

    c.   Self-esteem

N.   Coping strategies (how are feelings handled/personality style)

1.   Defenses (intellectualize, repress, project)

2.   Support systems

3.   Previous therapy

    a.   When

    b.   What type(s)

    c.   Reason(s)

    d. Duration, and reason for termination

    e. Results (what was gained)

    f. If prior sex therapy, describe

  O. Medical history

   1. Illness

   2. Surgeries

   3. Medications

   4. Sexually transmitted infections

  P. Drug or alcohol use/abuse assessment

III. Partner History

  A. Each member of the couple is asked about his or her own history following the format above

  B. However, during the history-taking, each client is also asked about his or her:

   1. Impressions of the partner

   2. Understanding of the partner's history including:

    a. Partner's current functioning

    b. Extended family relationships

    c. Any other information useful for understanding the other client through the eyes of the partner

IV. Concluding Comments and Questions

  A. "If there were one thing about yourself/partner you would like to change, what would that be?"

  B. "What is it that you most like about yourself/partner?"

  C. "Is there anything else you think I should know about you or the relationship that I have not asked?"

  D. End by reassuring that there will be ample opportunity to modify or add to information already presented.

Appendix B: Sensate Focus 1 Instruction for Clients©
Linda Weiner, MSW, and
Constance Avery-Clark, PhD

I. Purpose of Sensate Focus 1

    A. Teaching about sex as a natural function

        1. You cannot consciously make sexual desire, arousal, or orgasm happen

        2. You cannot keep sexual desire, arousal, or orgasm from happening

        3. The suggestions will teach you to get your conscious mind out of the way

        4. Allowing your body (which knows how to do these things) to take over

You do this by:

    B. *Touching for self-focused interest* rather than for a particular emotional or sexual response

        1. This means focusing on the touch sensations of temperature (cool or warm), pressure (firm or light; hard or soft), and texture (smooth or rough)

        2. You pay attention to these sensations for what they are without judgment or expectation. This is *mindfulness practice*

    C. *Touch for yourself* rather than for your partner

        1. Focus on your own sensations when touching or being touched

        2. Focus on the touch sensations that are present for you in the moment

    D. *Managing distractions.* When you find your attention going to anything other than touch sensations (which it will)

        1. You bring your attention back to these touch sensations

        2. Anything other than temperature, pressure, and texture is a distraction that is likely to trigger a goal-oriented mindset

        3. The most common distractions are expectations about emotions and responses you think you should have ("Am I going to get aroused?"), judgments ("Am I doing this right?"), and focusing on the other person ("Is my partner doing okay?")

    E. Learning that *touching can be intimate for its own sake*, as much if not more so than specific acts like intercourse

    F. Experiencing how *sexual responsiveness will arise naturally* from touch that is not goal-oriented but, rather, is sensory-oriented

II. Instructions for Sensate Focus

    A. Refrain from intercourse, oral sex, or self- or mutual stimulation to release during this period

    B. One partner initiates the touching session. Do this by saying, "I'd like to touch now"

    C. Partners take turns touching each other with the person who initiates touching first

    D. The other partner can decline the initiation but then it becomes that partner's responsibility to initiate the session at another time, and it still counts as the first partner's initiation

    E. Between one Sensate Focus session and the next, alternate who initiates the touching/touches first

    F. Arrange for one hour of complete privacy when you are not exhausted and not likely to be disturbed. (For example, make sure pets are not in the room and that the door is locked)

    G. Refrain from using alcohol or recreational drugs before or during Sensate Focus

    H. Refrain from using candles, lotions, music, or anything else that suggests an expectation of romance. This is not intended to be romantic but rather mindful

    I. Have a comfortable temperature in the room

    J. Have some light on in the room

    K. Have as little clothing on as possible, and no clothing is preferable

    L. Take off your own clothes. This is not a seduction but a mindfulness exercise

    M. Refrain from talking during the touching session

    N. You can assume any position that is comfortable for you and your partner

    O. Each person touches long enough to practice focusing on sensations and managing distractions by refocusing on sensations, but not so long you get very bored or tired. This is usually somewhere between ten and 15 minutes but don't watch the clock!

    P. Touching experiences should be made a priority two to three times per week, approximately every 48–72 hours

    Q. If touching sessions are not happening spontaneously, they can be scheduled ahead of time

    R. Touch with backs and palms of hands and fingertips. Refrain from full-body contact and kissing

    S. If the person being touched experiences anything physically uncomfortable, emotionally very uncomfortable, or ticklish, he or she non-verbally moves the partner's hand away from that area, or briefly handrides, placing the hand over or under the partner's. The person touching can return to that area later

    T. Positive handriding is added later to show the partner what is of interest in terms of touch, and is indicated by the person who is being touched placing his or her hand on top of or below the partner's, moving the partner's hand to areas that are of interest, and indicating the location, degree of pressure, and type of motion that might be explored

III. After the Touching Session
    A. You and your partner lie next to each other for a few minutes
    B. When sexual release or activity becomes an option, this takes place at some completely separate time from the Sensate Focus session
    C. Please talk little about the sessions at first until you can integrate the non-evaluative attitudes and skills offered
    D. After the session is entirely over, journal about the experience focusing on three questions:
        1. On what sensations was I able to focus, and where?
        2. What distractions did I experience?
        3. How did I manage those distractions? (Most helpful answer: I refocused on touch sensations!); and
    E. Bring this information to your next therapy session

Appendix C: Sensate Focus Special Instructions and Modifications for Different Dysfunctions[©]

Linda Weiner, MSW, and
Constance Avery-Clark, PhD

Along with addressing the specific dysfunction concerns delineated below, it is presumed that the therapist will also focus on any relevant, individual or relationship issues throughout treatment. What follows is an outline of significant modifications and special instructions for varied sexual dysfunctions.

I. Male Hypoactive Sexual Desire Disorder (HSDD)
    A. More mental and physical erotic stimulation alone (self-Sensate Focus and self-stimulation)
    B. The couple creates more mental and physical erotic stimulation together
    C. Cultivating fantasies
    D. Reading erotic, romantic, and/or informational material
    E. Viewing erotic, romantic, and/or informational material

II. Female Sexual Interest/Arousal Disorder (FSIAD)
    A. Self-Sensate Focus and self-stimulation
    B. Sensory-oriented bath or shower
    C. Tune into the body in other than sexual ways, e.g., physical exercise, mindfulness exercises, meditation, yoga, etc.
    D. Vibrator exploration alone
    E. Vibrator exploration with partner
    F. Education about the fact that for women sexual interest/desire may not precede sexual activity but may evolve after sensory, sensual, or sexual activity begins
    G. Manage negative cognitions, especially about body image
    H. Cultivate fantasies
    I. Read erotic, romantic, and/or informational material
    J. View erotic, romantic, and/or informational material

III. Erectile Disorder (ED)
    A. When genital touching becomes part of the homework, the partner is initially recommended to move away from an engorged penis and touch elsewhere until engorgement subsides (gaining and losing engorgement on purpose)
    B. Manage spectatoring using a code word; both partners change physical position and activity, and continue with the touching rather than stop
    C. Recommend client begins using PDE-5 inhibitors, like Viagra, Cialis, Levitra, etc.

Appendix C

    D.   Recommend client continues use of PDE-5 inhibitors, like Viagra, Cialis, Levitra, etc.

    E.   Recommend client immediately discontinues use of PDE-5 inhibitors, like Viagra, Cialis, Levitra, etc.

    F.   Recommend client eventually attempts to discontinue use of PDE-5 inhibitors, like Viagra, Cialis, Levitra, etc.

    G.   Client and partner decide on their goals regarding use of PDE-5 inhibitors, like Viagra, Cialis, Levitra, etc.

IV. Delayed Ejaculation (DE)

    A.   Either reduce or eliminate self-stimulation to orgasm

    B.   Relearning techniques for idiosyncratic masturbatory patterns that cannot be duplicated with partner stimulation

    C.   Sexual fantasy techniques

    D.   Include self stimulation exercises without partner and with or without sexually explicit material

    E.   PC muscle awareness exercises

    F.   Relaxation training

    G.   Use of vibrator with self-stimulation

    H.   Use of vibrator stimulation by partner

    I.   Education about the two stage model of ejaculation

    J.   Alternating partner stimulation with self-stimulation by any means

    K.   Self-stimulation or partner stimulation to high plateau level and then insertion close to the time of ejaculation

V. Rapid, Early, or Premature Ejaculation (PE)

    A.   Education about the two-stage ejaculatory process

    B.   Coronal Squeeze technique

    C.   Basilar Squeeze technique

    D.   Stop-Start exercises without partner present

    E.   Use of lotion or oil with self-stimulation

    F.   Use of masturbatory sleeve, such as Fleshlight

    G.   Stop-Start exercises along with partner manual stimulation

    H.   Use of breath to let go of tension

    I.   Other relaxation techniques

    J.   PC Muscle awareness exercises

    K.   Insertion with no movement

    L.   Insertion along with the techniques of Stop-Start communication between partners

    M.   Use of an SSRI as an adjunct to therapy

VI. Female Orgasmic Disorder (FOD)

    A.   Self-exploration and self-stimulation homework without vibrator

    B.   Use of vibrator for stimulation

    C.   Development of sexual fantasies

    D.   Reading erotica

    F.   Viewing erotic visual material

    Reading romance novels

    Viewing educational visual material demonstrating masturbation techniques

    Connecting to and letting go of PC muscles (Kegels)

I.   Female astride position with partner

J.   Acting "as if" being orgasmic, using pelvic movement and vocalization

VII. Genital Pain (Dyspareunia)/Penetration Disorder (Vaginismus)

A.   Confirm accurate diagnosis of Dyspareunia or Vaginismus with a physician

B.   Ensure client is in full control of all touching and physical activities, including insertion

C.   Accurate education about the cause and nature of Dyspareunia or Vaginismus, that it cannot be thought through voluntarily

D.   Frequent use of handriding and positive handriding

E.   Connect to and let go of PC muscles (Kegels)

F.   Experiment with different positions

G.   Use of graduated dilators while alone

H.   Couple utilizes dilators together

I.   Partner assists with arousal and/or orgasm prior to using dilators together or separately

J.   View a video on Dyspareunia or Vaginismus alone or with a partner

K.   Join an online Dyspareunia or Vaginismus support group

L.   PC muscle exercises

M.   Use of lubricant

N.   Utilize visualization techniques

O.   Use of Botox as an adjunct to other therapies

P.   Refer client with Dyspareunia or Vaginismus to a physical therapist as an adjunct therapy

Q.   Refer client with Dyspareunia or Vaginismus to a physical therapist for primary dilator work

VIII. Sexual Trauma

A.   Process sexual trauma before Sensate Focus homework for the couple

B.   Intermix trauma processing and Sensate Focus homework for the couple

C.   Use a variety of techniques to reduce anxiety and increase relaxation

D.   Refer to a physician for anxiety reduction medication

E.   The survivor engages in Sensate Focus him or herself before homework as a couple

F.   Use handriding to allow survivor to experience control

G.   The survivor initiates

H.   The survivor plans and controls the advancement of the Sensate Focus hierarchy suggestions

I.   The survivor identifies triggers and learns management techniques

J.   The survivor learns to deal with dissociation and its management

K.   The couple engages in relearning touch techniques, such as the "magic pen" (Maltz, 2012)

L.   The couple create new rituals that celebrate or mark the sacredness or specialness of their sexuality

References

Aanstoos, C. M. (2012). A phenomenology of sexual experiencing. In P. J. Kleinplatz (Ed.), *New directions in sex therapy: Innovations and alternatives* (2nd ed.), pp. 51–68. New York, NY: Routledge.

Agronin, M. E. (2014). Sexuality and aging. In Y. M. Binik & K. S. K. Hall (Eds.), *Principles and practice of sex therapy* (5th ed.), pp. 525–539. New York, NY: Guilford Press.

Althof, S. E. (2010). Sex therapy: Advances in paradigms, nomenclature, and treatment. *Academic Psychiatry*, 34(5), 390–396.

Althof, S. E. (2014). Treatment of premature ejaculation. In Y. M. Binik & K. S. K. Hall (Eds.), *Principles and practice of sex therapy* (5th ed.), pp. 112–137. New York, NY: Guilford Press.

Althof, S. E., Rubio-Aurioles, E., & Perelman, M. A. (2012). Standard operating procedures for taking a sexual history. *The Journal of Sexual Medicine*, *10*(1), 26–35. http://doi.org/10.1111/j.1743-6109.2012.02823.x.

American Psychiatric Association. (2003). *Diagnostic and statistical manual of mental disorders* (4th ed., Text Revision) (DSM-IV-TR). Arlington, VA: American Psychiatric Association.

American Psychiatric Association. (2015). *Diagnostic and statistical manual of mental disorders* (5th ed.) (DSM-5). Arlington, VA: American Psychiatric Association.

Apfelbaum, B. (1995). Masters and Johnson revisited: A case of desire disparity. In R. Rosen & S. Lieblum (Eds.), *Case studies in sex therapy*, pp. 23–45. New York, NY: Guilford Press.

Apfelbaum, B. (2000). Retarded ejaculation: A much-misunderstood syndrome. In S. R. Lieblum & R. C. Rosen (Eds.), *Principles and practice of sex therapy* (2nd ed.), pp. 205–241. New York, NY: Guilford Press.

Apfelbaum, B. (2012). On the need for a new direction in sex therapy. In P. J. Kleinplatz (Ed.), *New directions in sex therapy: Innovations and alternatives* (2nd ed.), pp. 5–20. New York, NY: Routledge.

Auteri, S. (2014). How chronic illness can affect sexual function. Retrieved March 15, 2016 from www.aasect.org/how-chronic-illness-can-affect-sexual-function#sthash.cARqJyjG.dpuf.

Avery-Clark, C. (1983, February). *Sensate Focus: Overview*. Material from presentation by Robert C. Kolodny, M.D., Postgraduate Training in Sex Therapy, Masters & Johnson Institute, St. Louis, MO. (Available from C. Avery-Clark, Ph.D., 7000 Palmetto Park Road, Suite 407, Boca Raton, FL 33433).

Avery-Clark, C. (1986). Sexual dysfunction and disorder patterns of working and non-working wives. *Journal of Sex and Marital Therapy*, 12, 93–107.

Avery-Clark, C., & Weiner, L. (2017, in press). A traditional Masters and Johnson behavioral approach to sex therapy. In Zoë D. Peterson (Ed.), *The Wiley handbook of sex therapy*. Malden, MA: John Wiley & Sons.

Bailey, J. M., Vasey, P. L., Diamond, L. M., Breedlove, S. M., Vilain, E., & Epprecht, M. (2016). Sexual orientation, controversy, and science. *Psychological Science in the Public Interest: Association for Psychological Science, 17*(2), 45–101.

Bancroft, J., Carnes, L., Janssen, E., Goodrich, D., & Long, J. S. (2005). Erectile and ejaculatory problems in gay and heterosexual men. *Archives of Sexual Behavior, 34*(3), 285–297.

Barker, M., & Langdridge, D. (2010). Whatever happened to non-monogamies? Critical reflections on recent research and theory. *Sexualities, 13*(6), 748–772.

Basson, R. (2000). The female sexual response: A different model. *Journal of Sex & Marital Therapy, 26*, 51–65.

Basson, R. (2002a). A model of women's sexual arousal. *Journal of Sex and Marital Therapy, 28*(3), 1–10.

Basson, R. (2002b). Rethinking low sexual desire in women. *British Journal of Obstetrics and Gynecology, 109*(4), 357–363.

Beemyn, G., & Rankin, S. (2011). *The lives of transgender people*. New York, NY: Columbia University Press.

Bell, D. M., Toplis, L., & Espie, C. A. (1999). Sex therapy in a couple with learning disabilities. *British Journal of Learning Disabilities, 27*(4), 146–150.

Bergeron, S., Rosen, N. O., & Pukall, C. F. (2014). Genital pain in women and men: It can hurt more than your sex life. In Y. M. Binik & K. S. K. Hall (Eds.), *Principles and practice of sex therapy* (5th ed.), pp. 159–176. New York, NY: Guilford Press.

Blumstein, P., & Schwartz, P. (1983). *American couples: Money, work, sex*. New York, NY: William Morrow.

Breyer, B. N., Smith, J. F., Eisenberg, M. L., Ando, K. A., Rowen, T. S., & Shindel, A. W. (2010). The impact of sexual orientation on sexuality and sexual practices in North American medical students. *Journal of Sexual Medicine, 7*(7), 2391–2400. doi: 10.1111/j.1743-6109.2010.01794.x.

Briere, J., & Runtz, M. (1988). Symptomology associated with childhood sexual victimization in a non-clinical sample. *Child Abuse and Neglect, 12*, 51–59.

Brotto, L. A., & Heiman, J. R. (2007). Mindfulness in sex therapy: Applications for women with sexual difficulties following gynecologic cancer. *Sexual and Relationship Therapy, 22*(1), 3–11.

Brotto, L., & Luria, M. (2014). Sexual Interest/Arousal Disorder. In Y. M. Binik & K. S. K. Hall, *Principles and practice of sex therapy* (5th ed.), pp. 17–42. New York, NY: Guilford Press.

Brotto, L. A., Bitzer, J., Laan, E., Leiblum, S., & Luria, M. (2010). Women's sexual desire and arousal disorders. *Journal of Sexual Medicine, 7*, 586–614.

Brotto, L. A., Seal, B. N., & Rellini, A. (2012). Pilot study of a brief cognitive behavioral versus mindfulness-based intervention for women with sexual distress and a history of childhood sexual abuse. *Journal of Sex & Marital Therapy, 38*(1), 1–27.

Carvalheira, A. A., Brotto, L. A., & Leal, I. (2010). Women's motivations for sex: Exploring the DSM-IV-TR criteria for hypoactive sexual desire and female sexual arousal disorders. *Journal of Sexual Medicine, 7*, 1454–1463.

Castleman, M. (2011). Sex and chronic illness: Think that your medical diagnosis means an end to your love life? Think again. Retrieved March 13, 2016 from www.aarp.org/relationships/love-sex/info-03-2011/sex-help-chronic-illness.html.

References

Castleman, M. (2012). Great sex without intercourse: Older couples can look forward to trying out these creative alternatives. Retrieved April 11, 2016 from www.aarp.org/home-family/sex-intimacy/info-12–2012/great-sex-without-intercourse.html.

Center for Disease Control and Prevention. (2015, February 23). Diagnoses of HIV infection in the United States and Dependent Areas, 2013. Retrieved April 12, 2016 from https://blog.aids.gov/2015/02/cdcs-2013-hiv-surveillance-report-now-available-online.html.

Chivers, M. L., & Bailey, J. M. (2005). A sex difference in features that elicit genital response. *Biological Psychology*, *70*, 115–120.

Cohn, R. (2011). *Coming home to passion: Restoring loving sexuality in couples with histories of childhood trauma and neglect*. Santa Barbara, CA: ABC-CLIO.

Colebunders, B., De Cuypere, G., & Monstrey, S. (2015). New criteria for sex reassignment surgery: WPATH standards of care (Version 7, revisited). *International Journal of Transgenderism*, *16*(4), 222–234.

Courtois, C. (2016). Sexual concerns and dysfunction related to past sexual trauma. In S. Levine, C. Risen, & S. Althof (Eds.), *Handbook of clinical sexuality for mental health professionals*, pp. 181–194. New York, NY: Routledge.

de Botton, A. (1998). *How Proust can change your life*. New York, NY: Vintage.

De Villers, L., & Turgeon, H. (2005). The uses and benefits of "sensate focus" exercises. *Contemporary Sexuality*, *39*(11), i–vi.

Diamond, B. (n.d.). When one twin is born lifeless, mom and dad witness a true miracle. Retrieved June 12, 2016 from Little Things at www.littlethings.com/ogg-twins-miracle/?utm_source=LTts&utm_medium=Facebook&utm_campaign=babies.

Dodson, B. (1996). *Sex for one*. New York, NY: Three Rivers Press.

Edmond, T. (1999). The effectiveness of EMDR with adult female survivors of childhood sexual abuse. *Social Work Research*, *23*(2), 103–116.

Ellis, A. (2000). *How to stubbornly refuse to make yourself miserable about anything … yes, anything*. Ft. Lee, NJ: Lyle Stuart.

Enzlin, P. (2014). Sexuality in the context of chronic illness. In Y. M. Binik & K. S. K. Hall (Eds.), *Principles and practice of sex therapy* (5th ed.), pp. 426–456. New York, NY: Guilford Press.

Finkelhor, D., & Browne, A. (1985). The traumatic impact of child sexual abuse: A conceptualization. *American Journal of Orthopsychiatry*, 55, 530–541.

Fisher, A., & Fisher, S. (2016, April 14). Attachment and quality of life among consensually non-monogamous individuals. Presentation at *Challenging Ideology and Changing Perspectives –* 41st Annual Meeting, Society for Sex Therapy and Research (SSTAR). Chicago, IL.

Fisher, S. (2014). *Neurofeedback in the treatment of developmental trauma: Calming the fear driven brain*. New York, NY: Norton.

Flaubert, G. (1965). *Madame Bovary* (P. de Man, Trans.). New York, NY: W. W. Norton and Company.

Gallo-Silver, L. (2000). The sexual rehabilitation of persons with cancer. *Cancer Practice*, *8*(1), 10–15.

Gartrell, N. K., Bos, H. M. W., & Goldberg, N. G. (2012). New trends in same-sex sexual contact for American adolescents? [Letter to the editor]. *Archives of Sexual Behavior*, *41*(1), 5–7.

Graham, C. A. (2010). The DSM diagnostic criteria for female orgasmic disorder. *Archives of Sexual Behavior*, *39*(2), 256–270.

Graham, C. A. (2014). Orgasm disorders in women. In Y. M. Binik & K. S. K. Hall (Eds.), *Principles and practice of sex therapy* (5th ed.), pp. 89–111. New York, NY: Guilford Press.

Haines, S. (2007). *Healing sex: A mind-body approach to healing sexual trauma*. San Francisco, CA: Cleis Press.

Hall, K. S. K. (2016). Social trends and their impact on sexuality. In S. B. Levine (Ed.), *Handbook of clinical sexuality for mental health professionals* (3rd ed.), pp. 389–390. New York, NY: Routledge.

Hall, K. S. K., & Graham, C. A. (2014). Culturally sensitive sex therapy: The need for shared meanings in the treatment of sexual problems. In Y. M. Binik & K. S. K. Hall, *Principles and practice of sex therapy* (5th ed.), pp. 334–358. New York, NY: Guilford Press.

Heiman, J. R., & LoPiccolo, J. (1988). *Becoming orgasmic: A sexual and personal growth program for women* (Rev. ed.). New York, NY: Simon & Schuster.

Herman, J. (1997). *Trauma and recovery: The aftermath of violence from domestic abuse to political terror*. New York, NY: Basic Books.

Hertlein, K. M., & Weeks, G. R. (2009). Toward a new paradigm in sex therapy. *Journal of Family Psychotherapy*, *20*(2), 112–128.

Hollis, J. (1998). *The Eden project: In search of the magical Other*. Toronto, Canada: Inner City Books.

Iasenza, S. (2002). Beyond "Lesbian Bed Death": The passion and play in Lesbian relationships. In S. M. Rose (Ed.), *Lesbian love and relationships*, pp. 111–120. New York, NY: Routledge.

Iasenza, S. (2010). What is queer about sex? Expanding sexual frames in theory and practice. *Family Process*, *49*(3), 291–308.

IsHak, W. W., & Tobia, G. (2013). DSM-5 changes in diagnostic criteria of sexual dysfunctions. *Reproductive Systems & Sexual Disorders*, *122*(2) pp. 1–3, doi:10.4172/2161-038X.1000122.

James, E. L. (2011). *Fifty shades of grey*. New York, NY: Random House.

Jensen, S. B. (1984). Sexual function and dysfunction in younger married alcoholics: A comparative study. *Acta Psychiatrica Scandinavica*, *69*(6), 543–549.

Jindal, U., & Jindal, S. (2010). Use by gynecologists of a modified sensate focus technique to treat vaginismus causing infertility. *Fertility and Sterility*, *94*(6), 2393–2395. doi:10.1016/j.fertnstert.2010.03.071.

Jung, C. G. (1966). *Two essays on analytical psychology (The collected works of C. G. Jung*, Vol. 7, 2nd ed.) (H. Read, M. Fordham, G. Adler, & W. McGuire, Eds.) (R. F. C. Hull, Trans.). Princeton, NJ: Princeton University Press. (Original work published 1953).

Jung, C. G. (1990). *Symbols of transformation: An analysis of the prelude to a case of Schizophrenia (The collected works of C. G. Jung*, Vol. 5, rev. 2nd ed.) (H. Read, M. Fordham, G. Adler, & W. McGuire, Eds.) (R. F. C. Hull, Trans.). Princeton, NJ: Princeton University Press. (Original work published 1956).

Jung, C. G. (2009). *The red book: Liber Novus,* S. Shamdasani (Ed.), M. Kyburz, J. Peck, & S. Shamdasani (Trans.). New York, NY: W. W. Norton & Company.

Kaplan, H. S. (1974). *The new sex therapy*. New York, NY: Brunner/Mazel.

Kaplan, H. S. (1975). *The illustrated manual of sex therapy*. New York, NY: Quadrangle/New York Times.

Kaplan, H. S. (1987). *The illustrated manual of sex therapy* (2nd ed.). Routledge Taylor & Francis Group, New York, NY.

Kleinplatz, P. J., & Ménard, A. D. (2007). Building blocks toward optimal sexuality: Constructing a conceptual model. *The Family Journal: Counseling and Therapy for Couples and Families*, *15*(1), 72–78.

References

Kleinplatz, P. J., Ménard, A. D., Paquet, M.-P., Paradis, N., Campbell, M., Zuccarino, D., & Mehak, L. (2009). The components of optimal sexuality: A portrait of "great sex." *The Canadian Journal of Human Sexuality*, *18*(1–2), 1–13.

Konnikova, M. (2015, March 4). The power of touch. *New Yorker Magazine*. Retrieved April 10, 2016 from www.newyorker.com/science/maria-konnikova/power-touch.

Kristensen, Z. E., & Broome, M. R. (2015). Autistic traits in an Internet sample of gender variant UK adults. *International Journal of Transgenderism*, *16*(4), 234.

Laumann, E. O., Nicolosi, A., Glasser, D. B., Paik, A., Gingell, C., Moreira, E., et al. (2005). Sexual problems among women and men aged 40–80 years: Prevalence and correlates identified by the Global Study of Sexual Attitudes and Behaviors. *International Journal of Impotence Research*, *17*(1), 39–57.

Lee, C., Gavriel, H., Drummond, P., Richards, J., & Greenwald, R. (2002). Treatment of PTSD: Stress inoculation training with prolonged exposure compared to EMDR. *Journal of Clinical Psychology*, *58*(9), 1071–1089.

Leiblum, S. R., & Rosen, R. C. (Eds.) (2007). *Principles and practices of sex therapy* (4th ed.). New York, NY: The Guilford Press.

Lev, A. I., & Nichols, M. (2015). Sex therapy with lesbian and gay male couples. In K. M. Hertlein, G. R. Weeks, & N. Gambescia (Eds.), *Systemic sex therapy* (2nd ed.), pp. 213–234. New York, NY: Routledge/Taylor & Francis Group.

Lindau, S. T., Schumm, L. P., Laumann, E. O., Levinson, W., O'Muircheartaigh, C. A., & Waite, L. J. (2007). A study of sexuality and health among older adults in the United States. *New England Journal of Medicine*, 357, 762–774.

Linschoten, M., Weiner, L., & Avery-Clark, C. (2016). Sensate Focus: A critical literature review. *Sexual and Relationship Therapy*, *31*(2), 230–247.

McCarthy, B. W. (1973) A modification of Masters and Johnson sex therapy model in a clinical setting. *Psychotherapy: Theory, research & practice*, *10*(4), 290–293.

McCarthy, B. W. (2005) *Sex therapy for middle age and older adults*. Retrieved March 15, 2016 from www.apa.org/pubs/videos/4310727.aspx.

Maier, T. (2009). *Masters of sex: The life and times of William Masters and Virginia Johnson, the couple who taught America how to love*. New York, NY: Basic Books.

Maltz, W. (2012). *The sexual healing journey* (3rd ed.). New York, NY: HarperCollins.

Maslow, A. H. (1954). *Motivation and personality*. New York, NY: Harper and Brothers.

Masters, W., & Johnson, V. E. (1966). *Human sexual response*. New York, NY: Little, Brown and Company.

Masters, W., & Johnson, V. E. (1970). *Human sexual inadequacy*. New York, NY: Little, Brown and Company.

Masters, W. H., & Johnson, V. E. (1986). *Sex therapy on its 25th anniversary: Why it survives*. St Louis, MO: Masters & Johnson Institute. (Available from The Kinsey Institute for Research in Sex, Gender, and Reproduction, Indiana University, 1165 E. Third Street, Bloomington, IN 47405).

Masters, W. H., Johnson, V. E., & Kolodny, R. C. (1995). *Human sexuality* (5th ed.). New York, NY: Addison-Wesley Longman Publishers.

Meana, M., & Steiner, E. T. (2014). Hidden disorder/hidden desire: Presentations of low sexual desire in men. In Y. M. Binik & K. S. K. Hall (Eds.), *Principles and practice of sex therapy*, pp. 42–60. New York, NY: Guilford Press.

Melby, T. (2011). Trying to dance, but missing rhythm. *Contemporary Sexuality*, *45*(10), 1–7.

Mercer, C. H., Fenton, K. A., Johnson, A. M., Wellings, K., Macdowall, W., McManus, W., et al. (2003). Sexual function problems and help seeking behavior in Britain: National probability sample survey. *British Medical Journal*, 327, 426–427.

Metz, M. E., & McCarthy, B. W. (2003). *Coping with premature ejaculation: How to overcome PE, please your partner & have great sex*. Oakland, CA: New Harbinger Publications, Inc.

Metz, M. E., & McCarthy, B. W. (2004). *Coping with erectile dysfunction: How to regain confidence and enjoy great sex*. Oakland, CA: New Harbinger Publications, Inc.

Metz, M. E., & McCarthy, B. W. (2012). The Good Enough Sex (GES) model. In P. J. Kleinplatz (Ed.), *New directions in sex therapy: Innovations and alternatives*, pp. 213–229. New York, NY: Routledge.

Michaels, M. A., & Johnson, P. (2006). *The essence of Tantric sexuality*. Woodbury, MN: Llewellyn Publications.

Mona, L. R., Syme, M. L., & Cameron, R. P. (2014). A disability-affirmative approach to sex therapy. In Y. M. Binik & K. S. K. Hall (Eds.), *Principles and practice of sex therapy* (5th ed.), pp. 457–481. New York, NY: Guilford Press.

Montgomery, S. A., Baldwin, D. S., & Riley, A. (2002). Antidepressant medications: A review of the evidence for drug-induced sexual dysfunction. *Journal of Affective Disorders*, *69*(1–3), pp. 119–140.

Nelson, T. (2008). *Getting the sex you want: Shed your inhibitions and reach new heights of passion together*. Beverly, MA: Quiver, Quayside Publishing Group.

Nichols, M. (1982). The treatment of inhibited sexual desire (ISD) in lesbian couples. *Women & Therapy*, *1*(4), 49–66. doi:10.1300/J015V01N04_07.

Nichols, M. (2014). Therapy with LGBTQ clients: Working with sex and gender variance from a Queer Theory Model. In Y. M. Binik & K. S. K. Hall (Eds.), *Principles and practice of sex therapy* (5th ed.), pp. 309–333. New York, NY: Guilford Press.

Ogden, G. (2001). Integrating sexuality and spirituality: A group approach to women's sexual dilemmas. In P. J. Kleinplatz (Ed.), *New directions in sex therapy: Innovations and alternatives*, pp. 322–346. Philadelphia, PA: Brunner- Routledge.

Ogden, G. (2013). *Expanding the practice of sex therapy: An integrative model for exploring desire and intimacy*. New York, NY: Routledge.

Perel, E. (2007). *Mating in captivity*. New York, NY: HarperCollins.

Perelman, M. A. (2009). The sexual tipping point: A mind/body model for sexual medicine. *Journal of Sexual Medicine*, *6*(3), 227–632. http://doi.org/10.1111/j.1743-6109.2008.01177.x.

Perelman, M. A. (2014). Delayed ejaculation. In Y. M. Binik & K. S. K. Hall (Eds.), *Principles and practice of sex therapy* (5th ed.), pp. 138–155. New York, NY: Guilford Press.

Perelman, M. A. (2016). Why the Sexual Tipping Point® Model? *Current Sexual Health Reports*, *8*(1), 39–46. http://doi.org/10.1007/s11930-016-0066-1.

Perelman, M. A., & Rowland, D. (2006). Retarded ejaculation. *World Journal of Urology*, *24*(6), 645–652.

Pillai-Friedman, S. (2010). EMDR protocol for treating sexual dysfunction. In M. Luber (Ed.), *Eye movement desensitization reprocessing: EMDR scripted protocols*, pp. 151–166. New York: NY, Springer Publishing Co.

Price, J. (2015). *The ultimate guide to sex after fifty: How to maintain – or regain – a spicy, satisfying sex life*. Berkeley, CA: Cleis Press.

References

Puppo, V. (2013). Sexual dysfunctions induced by stress of timed intercourse and medical treatment. *BJU International*, 111(5), E267–E269. doi:10.1111/bju.12128_8.

Reddy, D. N. (2016). Love hormones: The nature and function of love. 48th Annual Conference of the American Association of Sexuality Educators, Counselors, and Therapists: Putting the Pieces Together: Inclusivity in Practice, San Juan, Puerto Rico.

Resnick, S. (2012). *The heart of desire: Keys to the pleasures of love*. Hoboken, NJ: John Wiley & Sons, Inc.

Richters, J., de Visser, R., Rissel, C., Grulich, A., & Smith, A. (2008). Demographic and psychosocial features of participants in bondage and discipline, "sadomasochism" or dominance and submission (BDSM): Data from a national survey. *Journal of Sexual Medicine*, 5(7), 1660–1668.

Robbins, C., Schick, V., Reece, M., Herbenick, D., Sanders, S. A., Dodge, B., & Fortenberry, J.D. (2011). Prevalence, frequency, and associations of masturbation with partnered sexual behaviors among US adolescents. *Archives of Pediatric and Adolescent Medicine*, 165(12), 1087–1093.

Robbins, J. (2000). On the track with neurofeedback. A new treatment may help with problems from ADD to depression, sleep disorders and epilepsy. *Newsweek*, 135(25), 76.

Rosen, R. C., Miner, M. M., & Wincze, J. P. (2010). Erectile dysfunction. In Y. M. Binik & K. S. K. Hall (Eds.), *Principles and practice of sex therapy* (5th ed.), pp. 61–85. New York, NY: Guilford Press.

Rosen, R. C., Miner, M., & Wincze, J. P. (2014). Erectile dysfunction: Integration of medical and psychological approaches. In Y. M. Binik & K. S. K. Hall (Eds.), *Principles and practice of sex therapy* (5th ed.), pp. 61–85. New York, NY: Guilford Press.

Sanders, J. D., & Sprenkle, D. H. (1980). Sexual therapy for the post coronary patient. *Journal of Sex & Marital Therapy*, 6(3), 174–186.

Sandfort, R., & de Keizer, M. (2001). Sexual problems in gay men: An overview of empirical research. *Annual Review of Sex Research*, 12, 93–120.

Seman, J. (1956). Premature ejaculation: A new approach. *Southern Medical Journal*, 49, 353–358.

Shapiro, F. (2001). *Eye movement desensitization and reprocessing: Basic principals, protocols, and procedures*. New York, NY: Guilford Press.

Shaw, J. (2014). Approaching your highest sexual function in relationships: A reward of age and maturity. In Y. M. Binik & K. S. K. Hall (Eds.), *Principles and practice of sex therapy* (5th ed.), pp. 175–194. New York, NY: Guilford Press.

Sieber, J. (2012). Transgender transitions: Sex/gender binaries in the digital age. *Journal of Gay & Lesbian Mental Health*, 16, 74–99.

Tepper, M. S. (2000). Sexuality and disability: The missing discourse of pleasure. *Sexuality and Disability*, 18(4), 283–290. doi:10.1023/A:1005698311392.

Tepper, M. S. (2015). *Regain that feeling*. North Charleston, SC: CreateSpace Independent Publishing Platform.

Tiefer, L. (1991). Historical, scientific, clinical and feminist criticisms of "the human sexual response cycle" model. *Annual Review of Sex Research*, 2, 1–23.

Van der Kolk, B. (2014). *The body keeps the score: Brain, mind and body in the healing of trauma*. New York, NY: Viking.

Weeks, G. R., & Gambescia, N. (2009). A systematic approach to sensate focus. In K. M. Hertlein, G. R. Weeks, & N. Gambescia (Eds.), *Systematic sex therapy*, 341–362. New York, NY: Routledge.

Weiner, L. (1988). Issues in sex therapy with survivors of intrafamily sexual abuse. *Journal of Women in Therapy*, 7(2/3), 253–264.

Weiner, L., & Avery-Clark, C. (2013, June). *The art of Sensate Focus: Revisited and revised in contemporary times*. Poster session presented at the 45th Annual Conference of the American Association of Sexuality Educators, Counselors, and Therapists: Embracing the Sensuality of Diversity in Identities and Culture, Miami, FL.

Weiner, L., & Avery-Clark, C. (2014). Sensate Focus: Clarifying the Masters and Johnson's model. *Sexual and Relationship Therapy, 29*(3), 307–319.

Weiner, L., & Stiritz, S. (April 2014) Sensate Focus today: Results of a survey of current practitioners. Poster session presented at the 38th Annual Meeting of the Society for Sex Therapy and Research: From Complexities and Contradictions to Health and Happiness, Pittsburgh, PA.

Weiner, L., Cannon, N., & Avery-Clark, C. (2014). Reclaiming the lost art of Sensate Focus: A clinician's guide. *Family Therapy Magazine, 13*(5), 46–48.

Weitzman, G. D. (1999, March 12). What psychology professionals should know about polyamory: The lifestyles and mental health concerns of polyamorous individuals. Based on a paper presented at the 8th Annual Diversity Conference, Albany, New York, NY.

Zoldrod, A. (2015). Sexual issues in treating trauma survivors integrating the psychosocial. *Current Sexual Health Reports, 7*(1), 3–11.

Index

Note: illustrations are denoted by *italicised* page numbers

Index